Becoming Self-Reliant

How to Become Less Dependent on Society and the Government

By Ken Larson

Becoming Self-Reliant–How to Become Less Dependent on
Society and the Government

Copyright © 1999 by Rhema Publishing, Inc.

To reorder: Write Rhema Publishing, Inc. P.O. Box 789,
Suwanee, GA 30024. Phone: 770-932-6991. Cost $12.95.
Postage and Handling: First book $2.00. Additional books
$1.00 each.

Library of Congress Cataloging and Publication Data

Larson, Ken
  Becoming Self-Reliant - How to Become Less Dependent on
  Society and the Government
  Includes index.
  1. Survival Skills 2. Homesteading 3. Gardening
  4. Disaster Skills

ISBN 0-9642497-1-5

TABLE OF CONTENTS

Chapter I   **How and Where to Store Precious Water**   11

Storage Containers, Preparation for Water
Storage, Storage Precautions, Other Water
Storage Tips, Additional Water Sources,
Purifying Water, and Conservation.

Chapter II   **Food Storage–Learn How and What to**   29
                   Store Before You Need It

Food Shortages, Food Storage, Extending
Food Inventory, Savings and Return on
Investment, Two–Pantry Inventory System,
Sample Food Inventory List, and Emergency
Evacuation Provision.

Chapter III   **Bulk Commodities and Low Moisture**   47
                    Foods

Bulk Commodities, The Basics for One
Adult–One Year, Self Stable Foods,
Gardening and Foraging, Shelf Life, Food
Reserve Considerations, and Barter Items.

Chapter IV   **Bartering for Goods and Food**   57

Chapter V   **Drying Foods at Home**   59

The Drying Process, Food Spoilage, Drying
Equipment, Drying Methods, Preparation of
Vegetables for Drying,

Preparation of Fruits for Drying,
Conditioning, Pasteurizing, Packaging and
Storing, Preparing Dried Foods for Table
Use, and Nutritive Value of Dried Foods.

Chapter VI   **Rabbits–A Proven Meat You Can
Raise Anywhere**   85

Breeds, Housing, Disease and Injury,
Feeding and Watering, Nest Boxes,
Breeding, Pregnancy, Kindling, and
Butchering.

Chapter VII   **Pigeons–Unusual Urban Survival**   101
Meat Source

Facilities, Enemies, Pigeon Lofts,
Care, Breeds, Sex, Nest Boxes,
Perches, Feeds, Water, and Grit.

Chapter VIII **How to Use Fish Traps**   133

Fish Traps, Trap Baits, Trap
Locations, Trap Wings, and Trap
Types.

Chapter IX   **Nature's Free Foods**   131

Eating Wild Foods, Cattails,
Grapes, and Greenbrier.

Chapter X   **How to Use Insects as Food**   147
Insect Nutrition, Edible Insects
and Preparation Basics

Chapter XI   **Self-Sufficiency**   159
When Power Goes Out, Animal Feed
Grade Grains, Spartain Gain Storage
System, Recipes, Multi-grain Breads,
Box Cooking, Diatomaceous Earth,
Storing Eggs and Water Saving Methods

Chapter XII   **Utilities**   193
Coleman Lighting, Amperage Table,
Kerocene Lamps and Propane Lights
and Appliances

Chapter XIII **Fuel Storage**   204

Chapter XIV **The Narrow Hole Latrine**   209

Chapter XV   **Looting - Neighbors Cruising for
Your Goods**   211

Appendix A   **A Personal Note from Ken**   217

Appendix B   **Fish Trap Construction Plans**   222

Appendix C   **Home Drying of Vegetables
and Fruit**   225
Index   229

PREFACE

As we look at our world today, our future seems uncertain. As we focus our attention on America and Europe, we see a cloudy economic horizon. Yet most of us haven't taken much action to make preparations for economic collapse, food shortages, or major disasters. Others are now warning of difficult times ahead:

> **"Prepare for economic collapse - Those unprepared may stand naked before a crisis unseen in the United States since the civil war."**
> Pat Robertson - President of CBN

> **Be Prepared For Hard Times Ahead: "A days wages for a loaf of bread"** ... **"A wise man sees things ahead and prepares for them."**
> Proverbs 2:4, 22:3

> **"America faces its greatest financial crises in history during the 1990's."**
> Larry Burkett, author of *The Coming Economic Earthquake*

> **"It's not a question of when but how soon there will be a food crisis."**
> Frank Ford, author of *The Coming Food Crisis*

During the last few years, many have begun to simplify their lives, to reduce their debts, and to be less dependent on a fragile society for all their physical needs. Unfortunately, however, most people do not have sufficient knowledge or skills required for living simply.

As a disaster analyst with the Federal Government, I regularly see instances of our food system collapsed and our unprepared population reacting in panic to a shortage situation. During recent disasters, I have seen fights break out in grocery stores between good people over water for sale at $10.00 a gallon, ice at $15.00 a bag, and candles marked up 500 percent. Prepared people would not depend on these things.

Here is a scenario of what could happen.

A typical family wakes up to an alarming report on the radio. *"The New York stock market opened down 150 points and still falling. Gold vendors are swamped with orders."*

Amazement sweeps over them as they look at each other. Could this be the collapse foretold by those "doom and gloom" writers. Their thoughts are interrupted by the next flash. *"Foreign banks have withdrawn massive deposits from U.S. banks. The banking system is in a panic."*

Trying to maintain his composure, the husband decides to drive to the bank while his wife goes to the grocery store to stock up. He will meet her there once he gets some cash from the savings account.

When he arrives, the line reaches around the bank. Once in line, he feels the fear around him.

A passing motorist announces that a national emergency has been declared and all banks are temporarily closed and all transfer of funds will cease. No checks, not credit, and even the ATM's are closed.

The husband's heart sinks when he realizes they have almost no cash, minimum gasoline, and very little food in their pantry.

John drives to meets his wife, who is crying while waiting at the grocery store. Others had beat them there and the shelves were empty. "What will we do? Why didn't we stash a little extra cash and food?" she cries. "What will our $20 buy. Even the gas stations are already out of gasoline and are closed," he says.

As they head for home, they hear more news of bank defaults and third world countries defaulting on their debts. The stock market has closed as stocks continue to spiral downward. Gold is skyrocketing.

The following day, most businesses are closed while local bars are packed. There is now no water pressure and electricity is intermittent. Already, groups are roaming the streets looking for food and money. The family is now terrified. What happened to their comfortable world?

We have indeed lost many of the "basics" known and practiced by our forefathers. Too many believe all is well and have become totally dependent on their government for subsistence and help during emergencies. We have become dependent on a very fragile system which is generally not operated in our best interest. There is a need to return to a respectful knowledge of the land, learning self-reliant skills, and to frugal practices of storing consumable goods and barter items.

Ken Larson

BIOGRAPHY: Ken Larson

Ken Larson, a Disaster Analyst with the Federal Government lives near Atlanta, Georgia.

He has always been fascinated with survival techniques and his interest later increased during his outdoor experiences while hunting in north Alabama's hill country. Military training and a tour in Viet Nam spurred his fervent pursuit.

Ken often deals with victims of major disasters and has recorded secrets of their survival. In addition, he has sought out people who "live off the land" in rural areas across the country while continuing to expand his own preparedness skills. His series of family preparedness and survival articles for national magazines share his expertise.

He has produced several recent books:

Nuclear Emergency *– How to Protect Your Family from Radiation*

God's Free Harvest *– Successful Harvesting of Nature's Free Foods*

Becoming Self-Reliant *– How to be Less Dependent on Society and the Government*

Nature's Free Pharmacy *– Home Remedies Using Nature's Free Herbs*

Ken offers a comprehensive source of knowledge with a realistic approach to urban family preparedness. He received his BA and MBA from Auburn University. He and his wife Sandy, a CPA with her own private practice, have two children, Stacey and Brandon, and three grandchildren.

CHAPTER I

HOW AND WHERE TO STORE PRECIOUS WATER

Water is much more important for survival than food! Many have lived up to thirty days with no food, but chances of survival after four days without water are slim. We tend to underestimate how much water is actually needed not only for drinking but also for performing important routine tasks of daily living such as bathing, cooking, flushing toilets, cleaning eating utensils, and washing clothes. Most authorities suggest that a minimum of two gallons per day is required per person. This allotment includes one half gallon for drinking. Even as we are normally unaware of our actual water usage, we tend to take our water supply for granted. It is, in fact, very delicate.

Water shortage is almost inevitably a problem in a disaster. In every crisis situation, the majority of the general population is totally unprepared for even a small interruption in normal utility services. The victims expect and sometimes demand that "someone" provide them water along with protection, shelter, and food.

The most common disruption in water supply is due to a lack of electricity. With out electricity, there can be no water from purification plants or electrically powered wells. The second most disruption is due to a water main rupture. Recently, more than 10,000 people in the southeastern United States were without water for over two weeks due to such a rupture, and during Hurricane Hugo, many were without water for several months.

People who do not rely on public utilities for their water also suffer problems in a disaster, especially since most rural wells operate by public electricity. (In my own system, for example, a power outage shuts down the well unless I use a generator, which requires gasoline.) Well pumps become damaged, and wells often become contaminated due to flooding. Even non-disaster situations such as well-pump maintenance problems sometimes require well-users to seek other sources of water, and freezing weather also takes its toll on well pipes as well as city water lines.

During a disaster, local streams are not safe because of sewage and polluted surface water entering the watersheds. Drowned animals upstream may pollute the water downstream. Large bodies of water can have natural or manmade pollution. For example, during a recent hurricane, the wind blew foliage into a county's primary reservoir, causing the water to turn yellow and have an objectionable taste from the decomposing matter. This condition lasted for three weeks, affecting thousands.

A water shortage can happen quickly, but water deprivation can be minimized if an emergency supply of water has been previously stored. Fortunately, water stores well in a variety of containers.

WATER STORAGE CONTAINERS

If there is advance notice of a coming water emergency or any possible disaster, one should store as much water as possible. Fill up extra empty milk cartons, jars, bathtubs, sinks, wading pools, trash cans, and any other available containers.

Victims needing water wait in line for hours.

Drinking water can be stored in old rinsed out bleach bottles and plastic milk jugs. Some authorities report possible fracture of milk jugs with several years of age, but this fragility does not offset their convenience. I have had only a few jugs leak in many years of use. More durable containers are plastic 2-liter soda bottles. Five gallon buckets commonly used by restaurants are excellent for storing drinking water.

Larger containers are preferable for water to be used in dishwashing, toilet flushing, washing clothes, bathing, etc. Nicely serviceable larger plastic containers include five-gallon drywall buckets and thirty-gallon covered plastic trash containers. Unfortunately, since these are not originally intended for food contact, they may leach undesirable chemicals into the reserve to make it unsuitable for drinking.

Even if containers aren't available, expedient holders can be devised. For instance, plastic sheets or bags can be used to line porous containers for emergency drinking water storage. Even a depression dug in the ground and lined with plastic can be used to hold water on a temporary basis.

If the reserve supply should get low, water may have to be transported in. A five-gallon drywall bucket works well for this purpose, but any container used for water transportation should be closed to reduce spillage. Before I realized the importance of covered containers, I decided to transport water in several open buckets in the back of my truck. Even though I drove slowly, a third of the water sloshed out. I now keep extra plastic buckets, with lids, stacked in my storage room for last minute filling and for emergency transportation.

Water stores well in milk jugs in a dark area.

Once water is accumulated, a control method must be set up. An effective inventory begins with dating each container by permanent marker. Then water usage should be programmed on a first-in-first-out basis. All used water must be diligently replaced. The entire inventory should be rotated every year and questionable water in storage marked for non-drinking purposes. Since I have extra storage space, I keep my aged water for flushing toilets, washing clothes, etc., during power

Bulk (non drinking) water may be stored in a variety of containers.

outages. My water reserve has proved advantageous many times in the last ten years though some of its stored nondrinking water is over eight years old.

WATER STORAGE PREPARATION

With containers collected and ready, provision must be made for protecting the water against the growth of micro-organisms during storage. To do so, one may add sixteen drops of unscented liquid bleach (4-6 percent sodium hypochlorite) per gallon of water. I suggest, also, storing an extra jug of bleach for emergency purifying of questionable water.

WATER STORAGE PRECAUTIONS

In taking advantage of the convenience, little cost, and ready availability of plastic containers, we must not overlook risks! Careful storing must include deliberate separation from fuels, pesticides, or similar materials. The vapors from such products can penetrate the plastic and contaminate the water. Finally, water should be stored in the dark to protect the plastic containers from sunlight deterioration and the water from algae growth.

OTHER WATER STORAGE TIPS

Water storage utilizing glass jars is another method suggested by the Utah State University Extension Service. I recall their instructions include sterilizing glass containers: "Fill clean fruit jars with water, leaving an inch of head space at the top of the jar. Place clean sterilized lids on the jar and process the water in a boiling water bath the way fruit juice is processed. Quart jars should be processed twenty minutes, two-quart jars, twenty-five minutes."

Storing water is a simple procedure, but it is the primary provision for weathering a crisis. Along with making provisions for storing water, one should also identify alternate water sources.

OTHER WATER SOURCES

Trapped water in house plumbing lines can provide several gallons of water. Whenever the water pressure goes off, house lines should be carefully shut off from the street. This action will prevent drawing in contaminated water or allowing secured water to flow back into the connecting municipal system. To gain access to this water, the faucet at the highest point in the house should be opened, then the faucet at the lowest level should be opened to drain the lines into clean containers. (I deliberately installed a faucet in my basement to provide for utilizing water from the lines that run under my house.)

Other sources of water often unrecognized include the toilet tank (not the bowl), which stores several gallons and is immediately available. A water heater tank holds thirty to forty gallons. To get a free flow of this water, a vacuum may need to be released by opening a hot water faucet elsewhere in the house. Sometimes the tank must be vented to drain, so its "pop off" pressure relief valve lever should be opened. (Preparedness will include routine checks of the water heater tank because it may contain a foot or more of sediment. This should be drained out by opening the faucet at the tank bottom, connecting a garden hose, and venting the tank to allow the water to flow.)

Another source of water may be a waterbed. However, because of the possibility of algaecide in the water and plastic chemicals being leached into the water, one must not drink water from this otherwise good source.

These containers store water for flushing toilets.

Owners of a swimming pool have an important source of good water. After one hurricane, a swimming pool in Florida served a whole neighborhood with water.

The owners set up a temporary shower in the backyard next to the pool for their neighbors who also carried water back home with them.

One of the most obvious sources is rain. To collect rain water, open buckets or barrels may be placed under rain gutter downspouts. For cleaner collection, the containers may be lined with plastic bags. The pipes may have to be disconnected or cut so the water can flow into the containers. The first few minutes of rain should be allowed to bypass collection since it will contain a lot of sediment. Another collection method can be fashioned from plastic sheets placed on a hillside or strung between trees (outside the leafline) to funnel water into prepared containers.

WATER PURIFICATION

Pollution can affect ice, snow, water in streams, and water in shallow wells, causing these sources to be unsafe. Even clear streams can have parasites in them. However, there are relatively simple methods of purifying water in an emergency. If water from an unknown source or one of unknown quality must be used, one must be aware that the following methods of purifying water do not guarantee the safety of the water but will reduce the risks involved.

To make the purification process easier, clear water should be used whenever possible. If sediment is present, it will settle out in time and the cleared water can be poured off. The unsettled water can be poured through a cloth or coffee filter for speedier processing. A novel method to clear up water is to use a cloth siphon arrangement. This calls for placing the cloudy water container several inches higher than the empty clean-water container with a rolled-up clean, dry piece of

The accepted method to purify water is by boiling.

cloth connecting them to provide a siphon effect. This is a very slow process, but it has merit as a filtration system.

Surplus Civil Defense water storage container used as trash can.

Boiling water is one of the safest methods of water purification, although it does not remove pollution. Water should be boiled for at least twenty minutes to insure that bacteria are killed. (An easily forgotten fact is that it takes heat to boil water, and a knowledge of how to start a fire with or without matches may be required!)

After being boiled, water tastes flat (as does aged water) because some air has been driven out. To add back the oxygen, the water can be poured several times from one container to another or shaken vigorously in a closed container. Another way to improve the taste is to add a small piece of non-resinous wood, a pinch of salt, or a piece of charcoal from a spent fire can be added to the sterilized water. Flavored drink mixes will help.

I prefer boiling as a purification method, for I have friends who became sick apparently from water treated with purification tablets and processed through commercial filters. Commercial filters combine active ingredients to filter and treat the water at the same time. Some brands may not be as effective as they claim.

Organic matter in the water increases the amount of chemical needed to purify questionable water, and the colder the water, the more time required for the chemical to work. Regular household chlorine bleach can be used. Sixteen drops of liquid bleach should be added to each gallon of clear water and twice that amount mixed with cloudy or sediment-filled water. Because bleach loses strength over time, the recommended amount should be doubled if the bleach is over a year old, and one should not rely on bleach more than two years old. If there is not a chlorine smell after thirty minutes, the process should be repeated until one becomes obvious, or the water should be discarded. The container may be left uncovered for several hours to reduce the bleach taste and make the water more palatable.

Water purification tablets can also be used. Readily available from sporting goods stores or military surplus outlets, the tablets may be too old to do any good, so one should check the expiration dates before buying them and regularly update his supply. Iodine tablets work better than bleach or halazone tablets for certain intestinal parasites, and they have a shelf life of three to five years while halazone tablets have a shelf life of only two years.

During a disaster, those unprepared depend on tankers for water.

Another method of purification is distillation. Here questionable water is boiled and allowed to condense into safe water. One distilling method is to force the water vapor escaping out of a tea kettle spout to enter an inverted milk jug. The water vapor will condense in the milk jug and run out a hole cut in lower side of jug into a collection pan set nearby. An alternate method is to run the water vapor through copper tubing (same as used in home plumbing) to condense the vapor into pure water. For quantity production, try to visualize a moonshiner's still with its coil of copper loops.

Experience gained in using a variety of methods to purify water during normal times would be invaluable in a time of shortage. In such a time one would also really appreciate conscientiously established practices of water conservation during times of plenty.

WATER CONSERVATION

The more water is conserved in an emergency, the less water will be needed from emergency storage. However, it may be foolish frugality in an emergency situation to ration drinking water–to deprive people of it may adversely affect their health. On the other hand, stored water for non-drinking purposes must be conserved stringently. There are a number of methods for conserving non-drinking water.

As a water conservation principle, several bricks placed in a toilet tank can reduce the three-to-four gallons normally used for each flush. Also, the toilet need not be flushed after each use–but care should avoid too much waste matter collecting for an effective flush; otherwise a second required flush would defeat the original purpose. Additionally one might want to build an outdoor toilet trench such as described in The Boy Scout Handbook or other publications.

Beer manufacturer donates packaged water for disaster victims.

Personal bathing and clotheswashing use precious amounts of water. The periods between baths or showers can usually be safely stretched. A Navy shower procedure may be practical: one turns on the water to wet down, turns off the water, soaps up, and then turns on the water to rinse off. If water is extremely limited, a sponge bath should be the rule. Water should not be wasted on washing clothing other than underwear. In an area with heavy dew, dirty clothes left outside overnight will pick up moisture thus reduce the amount of wash water needed. Surprisingly, a heavy dew will make a towel moist enough to use for a sponge bath. Articles of clothing can even be dragged in the dew to wet them before beginning the laundry.

Water must never be thrown away unless diligent research has determined no additional uses for it. Tub water is fine for flushing a toilet. Handwashing water can be saved and used for the initial clotheswashing. Even dirty water with sediment in it should be saved—most sediment will settle out in several days if the dirty water is left undisturbed, and the clearer surface water can be used again for non-drinking purposes.

Along with essential concern about conserving water, it is also imperative that water conservation must never become a reason for avoiding washing the hands when preparing food. Intestinal infections easily result from bacteria inadvertently nurtured in unsanitary conditions, and they spread rapidly. Intestinal infections rapidly dehydrate the body and cause severe health problems.

Forethought, with a little simple advance preparation for water shortage can make a great difference in the health and peace of mind of emergency victims.

This creative family has water diverted into a reserve tank before use.

CHAPTER II

Food Storage: Learn How And What To Store Before You Need It

History shows that during a natural calamity, many affected areas have gone weeks with no food. Although we do not like to think about it, our current food distribution system is fragile and vulnerable to interruption by natural disasters, economic unrest, and even transportation strikes. Should an effective distribution strike or civil unrest create a national disaster, food shortage would be catastrophic. Therefore, it is fortunate that during most natural disasters, only one area of the country is involved so that resources from other areas may be diverted to the need.

A domino effect occurs when there are shortages. For example, during a disaster there is often a loss of electricity. With no electricity to operate gasoline pumps, there is a shortage of fuel because those stations able to use a generator to run the pumps soon sell out. Without gasoline, people cannot drive to stores that still have food. Furthermore, there can be no chain saw operation without gasoline; therefore, with storm-downed trees blocking roads, there can be no gasoline deliveries. Of course, no electricity also means no refrigeration, and so on.

During one hurricane I experienced, victim families lost all their perishable food due to lack of refrigeration and ice. When ice became available, it sold for $20.00 a bag while chain saws sold for $1,500, and generators could not be bought at any price. Some areas were isolated for thirty days due to debris blocking the roads.

FOOD SHORTAGES

In a typical large crisis, grocery stores are boarded up. If a store does remain open, its shelves are stripped in a short time. Even those of us unaffected directly by such an event have seen the raid on grocery stores during severe storm warnings, and we can imagine what would happen if the general public suddenly became alerted as to a potential long-term food shortage, or if there were an effective trucker strike.

Unfortunately, we do not seem to have the cooperative and self-sufficient attitude that we like to think prevailed during the Depression in the 1930's. We now have people who shoot each other over a traffic violation or in a gas line or when family jealousy becomes intense, and it is frightening to project what might happen with such people in a high-stress food line.

During a disaster, the Salvation Army, the Red Cross, and local relief organizations usually perform admirably. Unfortunately, many victims never get help because they do not get word (no battery powered radio) of the relief station location while others, lacking transportation, are not able to reach these support agencies. Those who do, find themselves involved in long lines for long waiting periods, away from their families. I have seen victims wait hours for a hot meal or for limited basic staples only to receive a pittance in what was available for issue. Many times the food and supplies thus provided are not what was wanted.

Bulk beans can be stored in food grade containers or those with liners.

Other times, problems are compounded because a support agency does not have an identification check-off system to reduce hoarding. Families may send children several times through distribution lines to acquire more

than their share of provisions. Some people travel from
relief station to relief station getting what they can at each
stop. I once overheard a family brag that they had
acquired enough free food for the whole next year.

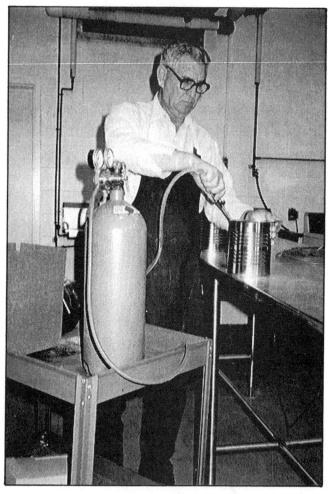

Nitrogen being added to stored food for insect protection.

Rural areas are normally inadvertently neglected by relief agencies. Despite hunting and fishing skills, many who consider themselves independent may have a false sense of security. Overtaxed sewers, flooding, and chemical runoffs can kill fish or make them unsafe to eat. Wild game may be severely depleted, and major changes in game habits occur during a large disaster such as a hurricane. During Hugo, much of the game moved from the area, and other areas had their local game population quickly depleted through poaching.

Recovery of a community following a disaster such as an ice storm or any long-term food shortage depends on how thoroughly the community is prepared. It should be obvious that we need to be less dependent on others to provide for us. Successful preparedness means that each family will have developed its own food storage plan.

A personal food storage plan is very important. Using a secondary "emergency" pantry is a good idea. Provisions for two weeks is minimal, but a several-month plan is better. Even storing an excess may become a means for helping a friend or neighbor. However, once a plan is effected, keeping the fact quiet may avoid "unwanted company" in a crisis.

A woman told me about her storm shelter to which she took her family when a tornado alert sounded to find it already crowded with her neighbors. Moreover, she said, they have regularly called on her to unlock the shelter for them, even in the middle of the night, whenever subsequent tornado alerts have been announced. I can envision a comparable "borrowing" of food from a publicized well-stocked emergency pantry.

FOOD STORAGE

Food may be stored many ways, but one of the most economical and readily effected methods uses regular grocery store items—packaged foods which

Bulk canning equipment is sometimes available at farmer's markets.

require no water for preparation and primarily those that can be eaten unheated. Dried beans and grain may be included, although they do require water for cooking and are subject to insect infestation unless properly stored in air-tight containers with an inert gas such as nitrogen.

Canned goods are appropriate since they are protected from exterior pollution; they should be wet-packed ones that one's family normally uses. Dented cans should be avoided.

Canned goods maintain nutrient values for one year before they are slowly depleted; therefore, they should be used–rotated out–annually, with no food kept for more than three years, and each can should be turned over every month to insure that the liquid coats all of the preserved product. (An angled storage rack that allows the cans to roll down as each is used will automatically perform this function.)

Inventory rotation is important. Using the oldest items first and moving the foods through the secondary pantry keeps items fresh and in reserve for the times when they may be needed.

Federal Emergency Management Agency (Civil Defense) publications claim that a two-week supply of emergency food will allow a family to get through 95 percent of most emergencies. One should begin a plan by listing the food items the family normally uses; then a menu is designed for a two-week period. Provisions should allow for a 2000+ calorie intake per day per person. The family survival inventory is made to accommodate the requirements and tastes; then items may be added for variety.

An emergency is a poor time to introduce unfamiliar foods or brands. I cringe each time I recall the first case of peas I bought as part of my storage plan. When it came time to rotate them out of inventory and into our main pantry, no one would eat them! They were not the brand we normally use. We ended up donating the cans to a church shelter.

A slanted surface automatically rotates stored can goods.

FOOD INVENTORY EXTENSION

Nutritious and cost-effective methods can be devised for extending a canned goods inventory. For instance, I have learned to enrich canned soups with rice, barley, and/or dried beans: two to four cups of cooked additive to a can of vegetable soup, with the required water, provides flavor, bulk, and carbohydrates for energy.

SAVINGS AND RETURN ON INVESTMENT

Storing foods makes good survival and economic sense. Bulk buying reduces cost and shopping time, and when one takes advantage of specials, even more can be saved. Stores specializing in bulk sales can be helpful, and sometimes a regular grocery store will reduce the unit price for case lots.

Also to be considered can be a return on investment due to inflation. If purchased goods are used the following year, any increase in prices due to inflation is a savings or return on one's investment. For example, if the price of the goods purchased goes up 10 percent over the next year, there is an untaxed gain of 10 percent on that food investment. This is a benefit of having the security of one's own food storage program and a tax free investment at the same time.

TWO-PANTRY INVENTORY SYSTEM

I recommend and use a two-pantry inventory system—the normal pantry is for regular daily meals and the other for a survival pantry. To follow this plan, one purchases all the items listed on the family's projected basic inventory. These are stored in an area separate from the normal pantry. It should be a dry place, if possible, at

A variety of containers are used to store food and staples.

optimum temperatures of 70 degrees or less since storage temperatures above this level reduce the foods' shelf life. With a magic marker or grease pen, items should be dated as they are purchased or entered into storage. The stored inventory list must be constantly updated.

A fringe benefit of the secondary "survival pantry" is that it becomes like the corner grocery store—one can go to it when the main pantry runs out of something. The "borrowed" item is put on the shopping list for the next trip to the supermarket, with a note that it is needed to replenish the survival provisions.

HERE IS WHAT TO STOCK

Many times we never get a project started because we become overwhelmed with the magnitude of the project. We all know a little is better than nothing. Toward this end, I would suggest beginning with a two week emergency plan. Most families can afford this level of investment and commitment for their future. Later you can expand up to a minimum of a three month inventory using the same pantry system.

Be sure to store some type of non-electric cooking device such as a propane stove. If possible, the stockpile should be kept somewhere other than the kitchen to help prevent dipping into it for day-to-day meals. If you do not have a basement, consider a portion of a bedroom closet, under a bed, or a top shelf that stores items never used anyway. Attics should not be used due to heat buildup or garages where freezing may occur.

The Miami Valley (Ohio) Disaster Services Office recommends foods storage for a two week period:

Water - Three gallons per person per day. See chapter on water storage for additional details.

Milk - Seven quarts (fluid) per person. Use nonfat dry milk or canned evaporated milk, figuring one tall can or 3 1/2 ounces dry solids mix per quart.

Canned meat, poultry, fish, dry beans and peas - 28 servings per person, including three ounces of meat, poultry or fish per serving; eight ounces per serving of meat mixtures (with macaroni, rice, etc.) and dry beans or peas; and half of a 10 1/2 ounce soup can per serving of condensed soups that contain the above foods.

Fruits and vegetables - 21 pounds of canned varieties, allowing 6-ounce servings of canned fruits or vegetables and 1 1/2 ounce servings of dried fruits.

Spread for breads or crackers - Stock according to family-use practices. Perhaps include cheese spreads, peanut butter, jams and jellies, syrup, honey, apple butter, relish, catsup, mustard, etc.

Cereals and baked goods - Five to seven pounds of ready-to-eat cereals, crackers, cookies, canned breads, steamed puddings or cakes, flour mixes, flour, macaroni, spaghetti, and noodles (both dry and canned dishes), allowing two ounces per serving.

Fats and vegetable oil - Use types that do not require refrigeration. Figure a pound or pint per person, depending upon the extent of cooking that is possible.

Sugars, sweets and nuts - One or two pounds, including white and brown sugars, hard candy, gum, nuts, and instant puddings.

This family cans the majority of their home-grown meat and produce.

ANOTHER SAMPLE FOOD INVENTORY LIST

(Family of four for 2 weeks)

	SHELF LIFE MONTHS	INV
WATER		
Gallons (Drinking & Misc.)	36+	6
MILK		
6-oz. cans evaporated milk	6	8
Lbs. powdered milk (Metal container)	6	4
MEAT		
1-lb. cans beef stew	18	6
1-lb. cans beef hash	18	6
12-oz. cans canned meat	18	12
FISH		
1-lb. cans salmon	12	2
7-oz. cans tuna	12	4
SOUP		
10 1/2 oz. cans cream soup	18	24
10 1/2 oz. cans vegetable soup	18	24
10 1/2 oz. cans consommé	18	16
Pkgs. (12) bouillon cubes	12	2
VEGETABLE		
17 oz. cans peas	18	6
17 oz. cans corn	18	6
28 oz. cans tomatoes	18	6
28 oz. cans green beans	18	4
1 lb. dried peas, beans, rice	24	10

FRUIT

45 oz. cans pears	18	4
45 oz. cans peaches	18	4

JUICE

46 oz. cans tomato juice	18	4
46 oz. cans orange juice	6	6
46 oz. cans grapefruit juice	6	6

CEREAL

Pkgs. cereal (instant)	12	2
Pkgs. ready-to-eat (10-12 boxes)	1	2

MISC.

40 oz. cans spaghetti/meat balls	18	4
18 oz. cans baked beans	18	4
12 oz. jars peanut butter	12	4
2 lbs. canned bread (date nut or brown)	24	12
1 lb. cans cookies	12	4
1 lb. cans crackers	12	4
2 lbs. sugar	Indef	2
8 oz. salt, spices	Indef	8
6 oz. jars instant coffee	18	2
1 1/2 oz. boxes instant tea	18	2
8 oz. boxes instant cocoa	18	2
3 oz. boxes instant puddings	12	6
2 lbs. hard candy	18	2
Pkgs. dried fruit	6	2
Btl. vitamins, mult, C, B complex	24	1
1 lb. protein powder	24	1

GENERAL INSTRUCTIONS

All foods should be in cans, jars, or tightly sealed plastic containers, preferably in sizes that can be used up for one meal. Select foods that will last without refrigeration and can be eaten with little or no cooking.

Commercially canned foods are best, especially the non-acid varieties (peas, beans, corn, etc.). The stock should include the special needs of infants, toddlers, the elderly, and those on limited diets.

Canned goods should have a number on them indicating their production and expiration date. If you cannot determine the dates by looking at these numbers, ask your grocer for help.

EMERGENCY EVACUATION PROVISION

An important addition to a second pantry is a crate or other container that can be used to carry provisions in an emergency evacuation. Plastic file boxes with sturdy tops are available at office supply outlets. About the size of laundry tubs, one of these can be packed quickly with foods that are high in calories, low in bulk, and light in weight to become a portable survival unit. I do not actually store food in mine, but I do keep one near my pantry. With it I have a packing list so I will not forget any of the essentials. It includes non-perishables such as plastic bags, can opener, etc., as well as foods that fall into the emergency category like powdered milk, nuts, oatmeal, hominy, cream of wheat, rice, spaghetti (whole wheat or spinach), and dried beans (and a reminder that many stored foods require water for processing).

CONCLUSION

A food storage system does require constant effort to be effective since the items must be replaced when they are used (it is very easy to "borrow" an item here and there and one day find one's inventory gone). Yet storing food for

Natural disasters, strikes, and riots cause the stores to board-up and close.

emergencies can become a rewarding enterprise even if disasters never demand using it. The value of stored food became especially clear to me once when I was out of work for a period of time and my survival pantry provided for my family through a very lean period.

CHAPTER III

BULK COMMODITIES AND LOW MOISTURE FOODS

For temporary emergencies, your emergency supplies of canned goods and everyday foodstuffs should be adequate. For major disasters and even an economic collapse, you may want to move into a longer term approach with additional supplies.

There are many schools of thought on long term food storage. I tend to divide them into two approaches. One is bulk commodities. It is an economical and a very basic approach using grains, salt, sugar or honey, oil or fats, milk powder, and legumes. The other is to buy low moisture foods such as dehydrated and freeze-dried foods.

Food storage programs for the most part are based on a balanced diet and a calculated daily caloric content. For example, 2,600 calories for adult males; 1,850 for adult females; 3,000 for teenage males, 2,300 teenage females, and 2,000 calories for children.

For a balanced diet, foods should be selected from all four food groups: meat, grains and fruit, dairy products, and vegetables.

It would be comforting to have a one year supply of food for each person in your family. In reality, most families begin with a one year supply for one person intending it to be divided among all family members.

When buying less than a complete package, it is better to buy smaller portions of all items rather than buying a years supply of one item If a need arises before all goods are purchased, a one years supply of limited goods will not be functional.

Care should be taken during extended storage of foods to maintain a dry and stable temperature of below 75 degrees. Heat will shorten shelf life whereas it can be extended under optimum conditions. A rule of thumb is for every 20 degrees increase, the shelf life of the food is decreased by one half.

BULK COMMODITIES

For many years the "basic four" of wheat, powdered milk, sugar or honey, and salt have been used to provide a very basic diet to sustain life at a Spartan level. Unfortunately, whenever someone eats the same food repeatedly, appetite fatigue develops. In some cases, they would rather starve than eat the same food again. Also, the psychological shock of disaster will cause many people to reject unusual foods and go hungry. This is especially true of young and older people. It has been documented that during war, many children and aged persons have starved to death rather than adjust to unfamiliar foods. During the potato famine in Ireland in the 1800's, millions died of starvation. Many peasants rejected corn, imported from outside the country, due to their dependence on potatoes as their primary staple. They felt corn was livestock feed! I seem to remember that even with wheat available, many men were seen that looked like thin, starving wolves roaming the land looking for food. We can learn from history. Under adverse conditions, we must try to make life as normal as possible.

So I have added several items to my food reserve such as legumes for additional variety and protein. I also recommend some grocery store canned goods, a supplement of vegetables (or grains for sprouts), and fruits as available. Variety is the key to your program.

Converting over to whole wheat is tough on one's internal system. Children can handle small amounts but not as the main basis of their diet. It is best to begin with everyday foods and begin to introduce new foods over a period of time. Try one new variation each week. This will allow you to learn how to use them and develop recipes you enjoy.

FOOD RESERVE CONSIDERATIONS

Determining your food reserve needs should be an informed process. On the other hand, a continual delay to gather every detail may insure that the reserves are never acquired. The following guidelines will give you a starting point. Remember, there is a wide variation in food reserve companies.

Look into the reputation and experience of the source and manufacturer. Do they offer guarantees. Familiarize yourself with the various types of foods available and the advantages and disadvantages of each. Compare cost per serving, quality, and size of portions. Most use the industry standard number 10 cans but they may have different content weight for the same food. So always compare weight, not just size or volume of the container.

Keep in mind the caloric and nutritional requirements of your family. Make sure your family will eat the food types supplied, and the calories are nutritional in value.

BULK STORAGE FOR EACH ADULT–1 YEAR

Grains–350 pounds: 2 cups of dry wheat per day.

Wheat is a primary item for any food storage program along with a good wheat grinder or mill. Most preparedness plans begin with hard winter wheat and then supplement with rolled oats, corn, and white rice (because of the bran, brown rice has a shorter shelf life). Wheat has a "stated" shelf life of 10-20 plus years. Oats and corn run 4 plus years where as popcorn is said to have the same shelf life as wheat. Popcorn also grinds into a good, healthy, gluten-free flour.

Normally bulk commodities (grains, beans etc.) are stored in sealed 5 gallon food grade plastic buckets filled with a nitrogen or oxygen absorber packet to kill insects. I use free 4 1/2 gallon buckets from Publix and Kroger bakeries. Contrary to some sources, tests show bay leaves will not kill insects. To use nitrogen, rent a small tank and purchase an helium regulator ($20) and have tank filled with commerical nitrogen at a welding supply company. Make a probe and insert into grain. To use dry ice, place 2 inches of grain in the bottom of a container and place approximately 4 oz. per 5 gallon bucket, then pour the rest of the grain on top. Lightly close the lid on the container (do not seal because of gas expansion) to allow the dry ice to evaporate. Tightly seal after 30 minutes. Since dry ice gives off carbon dioxide, it will fill the bucket. Dry ice available from large Kroger and Publix grocery stores. To test both methods for completeness before closure, a lighted match will go out when lowered into the bucket.

For an alternate method to kill insects or insect eggs in grain, place the bucket in the freezer (zero degrees) for seven days.

Grains can be ground into flour for breads or boiled mush, cracked (ground on coarse setting) into bulgur granules for cooked cereals, or spouted for greens.

GRAINS COOKING TABLE

Grain (1 cup)	Water	Time	Cooking Yield
Barley	3 cups	1 hour	3 1/2 cups
Bulgur	2 cups	20 min.	2 1/2 cups
Cornmeal	4 cups	30 min.	3 cups
Oats, rolled	1 1/2 cups	10 min.	2 cups
Rice, brown	2 cups	1 hour	3 cups
Rye	2 cups	1 hour	2 1/2 cups
Wheat berries	3 cups	2 hours	3 cups

Milk Powder–50 pounds. (Better: 85 pounds–
    Approximately 3 glasses of milk per day.)

Experiment with different brands. Many brands of long-term storage milk are much better than grocery store dried milk. Also milk tastes better the next day after making and is always good for cooking. If you like low fat milk, there should not be a problem with adapting to milk powder. Mixing with regular milk helps with the transition along with adding a small amount of vanilla.

Canned dried milk will store 15+ years with good nutrition but the flavor changes. Try chocolate or other flavorings to mask the taste. Do not stock if you do not like it–you will never use it and it will become rancid. If you do not store milk, find another source of calcium such as vitamin pills.

Sugar or Honey–30 pounds (Better: 100 pounds–One half cup per day.)

Harmful bacteria can't live in honey. Over time, honey will become granulated as it ages, or if stored at cold temperatures. This is a natural aging process. To bring the honey back to a liquid form, simply place the container of honey in a pan of warm water until the granules disappear. If more heat is needed, raise the honey's container off the pan bottom with a rack and away from the heat source. Honey in storage usually gets darker in color and stronger in flavor, but remains useful as ever. Sugar will get hard but it can be crushed into finer particles.

Salt–5 pounds

Many like to store extra salt for future bartering.

Legumes–100 pounds: Approximately 1/2 cup dried beans per day.

Legumes include all types of beans, peas, and lentils. To cook, first soak overnight and discard the water (lentils and split peas require no soaking). Then add the required amount of water, bring it to a boil, and cook. Adding salt to soaking beans and the discarding of water reduces both souring and stomach gases. Also start by eating a small amount at each meal and gradually increase your consumption each day to allow for your body to create enzymes to reduce gases.

Soybeans hold their shape more and do not become mealy as do other beans and they absorb other food's flavor when cooked together. To make a low cost meatloaf, mix 1/3 hamburger with 2/3 cooked and blended soybeans. Use this mixture as the meat source in your favorite meatloaf recipe and cook. Eat the next day after soybeans have absorbed the meat's flavor.

Legumes when combined with wheat or rice provide a "complete protein" including all the needed amino acids. Add legumes to salads, burgers, soups, and stews. Try a cold salad using cooked legumes, celery, tomatoes, vinegar, Mayo, and onion.

LEGUMES COOKING TABLE

Grain (1 cup)	Water	Time	Cooking Yield
Black beans	4 cups	1 1/2 hrs.	3 cups
Black-eyed peas	3 cups	1 hour	3 cups
Kidney beans	3 cups	1 hour	3 cups
Lentils	3 cups	45 min.	3 cups
Soybeans	4 cups	2-3 hours	3 cups
Split peas	3 cups	45 min.	3 cups

Oils and Fats–12 gallons: 1/2 cup of oil per day.

A good source of calories which will be difficult to obtain during difficult times. Store extra for bartering.

Vitamins

A good multiple vitamin along with extra vitamin A, C and B-complex. Add vitamin D for fast growing younger age groups.

Seeds for Sprouting–6 pounds

Kitchen gardening with spouts adds bulk and improves flavor of soups, salads, casseroles, and breads. Sprouting greatly increases vitamin content of dishes and replaces other greens that may be unavailable. To prepare, place seeds in a quart jar with two cups of warm water. Soak for 6-8 hours, or overnight. Secure a gauze or nylon fabric on the jar mouth with a rubber band and drain seeds. Place jar in warm, dark place. Rinse seeds at least 3 times each day and drain. On the last day place only alfalfa in the light (not the sun) to gain vitamin A and chlorophyll. When spouts reach desired length, remove and refrigerate until used.

Rinse mung beans and garbanzos more often and in warmer water. Be sure to drain well.

Additional Variety Foods

For basic cooking, add shortening, baking powder, yeast, baking soda, pepper, bouillon, chili powder, and 5 #10 cans of powdered eggs. Other good additions would be 10 pounds peanut butter, 100 pounds of canned meat or several #10 cans of dehydrated TVP (Textured Vegetable Protein), 100 pounds canned fruit, 50 pounds of canned vegetables, 2 #10 cans of powdered drink concentrates, 1 #10 can of tomato powder, 1 #10 can of dehydrated onions, and 1 #10 can of potato flakes. Good foods for children and your sanity are Jell-O, tapioca, puddings, cake mixes, hard candies, and chocolate chips.

ESTIMATED SHELF LIFE OF PRODUCTS IN NITROGEN PACKED CANS

PRODUCT	ESTIMATED SHELF-LIFE IN YEARS
Beans	10+
Corn	4+
Eggs	5+
Fruits	8+
Grains, Whole	10+
Granola	5+
Meat, Freeze-dried	5+
Milk–Non fat	8+
Nuts	4+
Oats	4+
Pasta	8+
Peas	8+
Popcorn	10+
Rice	4+
Sweeteners	10+
TVP–Textured Vegetable Protein	10+

SHELF STABLE FOODS

Dehydration (Most cost effective method)

Foods are passed through high temperatures for a period of time to remove moisture. Those foods that do well are corn, peas, carrots, mushrooms, bell peppers, onions, tomatoes, and fruits. In some limited cases, industry accepted preservatives are used. Best for those on a limited budget and just beginning food storage.

Freeze-dried (Most expensive method)

In many cases, freeze-drying retains the shape and texture better than dehydration. To freeze-dry, the food is rapidly frozen. The water content is turned into gas and removed during a vacuum and heating process. Normally no preservatives are used.

GARDENING AND FORAGING

Many find they like to supplement their program by learning to forage using nature's bounty. Turn to the chapter on Nature's Free Foods for a sample of wild foods.

CONCLUSION

Yes, food storage is truly a wise investment. I store extra for bartering and if I become overstocked or some items are maturing, I donate them to my city's homeless mission and take the tax write-off.

I once saw an Associated Press release where a scientist stated starvation would be the number one killer in the next world war. A few years ago the Social Security Administration predicted within the next 60 years, a $70.00 grocery bill (which only fifteen years ago was $25.00) will run over $1,500.00. By storing foods now, you hedge against inflation and shortages and those savings are tax free. So, invest in your future and not just in the bank.

CHAPTER IV

BARTERING FOR GOODS AND FOOD

During hard times, bartering becomes a way of life. The primary law of barter economics is supply and demand - High Bid Wins!

In *Black Market Money* by Walter Rundell, a study of post-World War II black markets in occupied nations in the American zone, he found market prices were one hundred times the legal prices for soap, butter, sugar, saccharine, coffee, flour, hosiery and flints. (Presumably prices were even higher earlier in the occupation.) Oleomargarine, liquor and eggs commanded prices seventy-five times higher; whereas potatoes and beef sold for fifty times more. Coal, gasoline, rubber tires, light bulbs, suits, and dresses sold for prices twenty-five times more than the legal limit.

In 1944, the Allied air invasion cut off the Holland's densely populated industrial west. The food rations were two pounds of sugar beets, two pounds of potatoes, and one loaf of bread per week per person. Bicycles were the only transportation. Because all rubber was confiscated months before, people pedaled on the bicycle rims looking for food. They took personal effects and anything they had to trade. Many who lacked strength, never made it back home to their families.

In 1947, during the shattered economy of Japan, soap and cigarettes became as valuable as gold. In one case, a soldier emptied his pockets of soap and cigarettes to make a trade. He received thousands of yen which bought a shoeshine, massage, ride, souvenirs, bar tab etc. with many yen leftover.

In 1974, in Cairo, Egypt, two people were killed and five injured in a rush to buy a piece of soap. During the same year in New Delhi, the government began a drive against hoarding. They raided shops, safety deposit boxes and homes for grain, paper, kerosene, soap, cigarettes and other fast-moving consumer goods. In Bombay, the favorite trading commodities were food, soap, toothpaste, and even combs.

We should learn from the past and pack away extra consumer goods for trading. Add to your list bar soap, laundry soap, shampoo, toothpaste, deodorant, wood matches, light bulbs, toilet paper, sanitary napkins, low cost used 22 rifles and ammunition, insect repellent, medicines for stomach problems and diarrhea, aspirin, toilet paper, disposable razors, Coleman lantern mantels, propane, gasoline, auto oil, and spark plugs. Try a mountain bike, moped, an extra set of extra tires for each, tire repair supplies,12 volt air pump, and extra bicycle tubes. You can even barter tire repairs for whatever else you need. Speaking of repairs, stock small hand propane tanks for plumbing, solder, flux, copper pipe and joints, hand tools, and the list goes on.

Learn skills that can be bartered. I even plan to use foraging skills as shown in my book *God's Free Harvest* to barter food items. I recall a quote from one starving unskilled refugee after unsuccessfully trying to sell his gold watch and rings for food. He said, "I found the skills of labor are worth more than precious gold."

Finally, you should store cash. It is always in short supply. During major disasters, I have found the small bills are best. Those who have something to sell have minimum change. For smaller items, everything rounds up to the nearest dollar.

CHAPTER V

DRYING FOODS AT HOME

INTRODUCTION

Drying foods at home is easy, different, fun, and not just for fruits anymore. Dried food is an alternative that is often overlooked as a means of food storage and self-reliance. Drying food is also a means of spicing up the daily menu with foods of different flavors and textures.

Ivon McCarty, Professor of Food Technology and Science at the University of Tennessee provided the input for this section.

There are basically three methods of drying: sun drying, oven drying, and drying in specially constructed dehydrators. The process is simple, but you will need to learn a few basic principles and improvise your own drying method.

Do not hesitate to use the trial and error approach. Make simple trays by fastening cheesecloth or screen mesh to shallow wooden frames or oven racks. After loading the trays with food, place them outside in the sun, in the attic, or in an oven to dry. Use small quantities of several foods when learning how to dry. Remember that all foods do not dry equally well nor do all drying methods produce similar results. Do not become discouraged if your first few attempts do not turn out as you expected.

Learning to cook with dried foods will be a new experience for many. Dried foods taste different from their fresh counterparts. You and your family will have to experiment to decide which dried foods you like best that fit into your garden mix.

THE DRYING PROCESS

The objective in preserving food by drying is to reduce the moisture level in the food to a point where bacteria, yeast, and mold can not grow. If moisture is not available, these microorganisms cannot grow and spoil the food.

Heat, low humidity, and moving air, working together, will dry anything–food, clothes or hair. Nature likes a balance. In order to equalize the moisture difference between a food and the air surrounding it, the dry air accepts some of the water from the food. If the surrounding air is humid, it cannot take on more moisture; therefore, the food will not dry and will spoil on the drying tray. If there is flowing air to carry away the moisture-laden air, drying can take place.

Low humidity and air movement are as important as heat when drying food. For example, clothes will dry outside in the dead of winter with snow on the ground if the air is dry. They will dry even more rapidly if the wind is blowing. Heat is important because warm air can hold more moisture than cold air. Each 27 degrees Fahrenheit increase in temperature doubles the amount of water the air can carry.

A temperature of 140 degrees Fahrenheit is recommended for drying foods. Higher temperatures cause the food to cook resulting in an internal breakdown of product structure and internal release of cell contents (sugars, starches, protein, and minerals). These contents move to the surface and form a hard crystalline layer which slows heat penetration and prevents moisture escape. The resulting food product will be dry and hard on the surface while still moist and soft on the inside. This is called "case hardening." If the temperature is too low, the food will dry too slowly and microorganisms may cause spoilage.

Air movement is essential to successful drying. However, if its flow is too great, it will reduce heat penetration into the product and prolong the drying time. The product surface will become dry and leathery, but the product may spoil from internal souring before it becomes totally dry.

FOOD SPOILAGE

There are two types of spoilage that must be dealt with when preserving food. One type of spoilage is caused by enzyme activity and the other type is caused by microorganisms such as bacteria, yeast, and mold.

Enzymes responsible for ripening fruits and vegetables continue to cause flavor and color changes until the food spoils. This ripening/spoilage action accelerates when fruits and vegetables are cut or peeled and exposed to air. For example, apples turn brown. When preserving food, it is essential that a pretreatment step be included to preserve quality. Blanching vegetables before drying is a must. Blanching in steam is the preferred method; however, water blanching is commonly used. Pre-treating fruits before drying is optional but necessary to prevent discoloration. Sulfuring is the most effective "commercial" pre-treatment for most fruits. It also aids in the retention of vitamins A and C.

Once the drying process begins, it should not be interrupted. This is essential in drying vegetables. Molds and bacteria will grow on partially dried vegetable held at room temperature, causing them to spoil. The sugars and acids in fruits make them less susceptible to spoilage. The surface moisture on the food must be removed quickly to prevent spoilage and loss of quality. This is why a higher temperature recommended when food is first placed in the dryer. The temperature will drop approximately 20 degrees Fahrenheit when moist food is placed in the dryer and prevent the food from overheating. When the food surface appears dry, the temperature should be reduced to 140 degrees Fahrenheit and maintained at that level throughout most of the remaining drying process to reduce the risk of case hardening and overdrying. The temperature should be further reduced near the end of the drying process to prevent scorching the food.

DRYING EQUIPMENT

The equipment necessary for drying need not be elaborate nor expensive. Equipment needs depend upon the experience and inventive nature of the user as well as the amount of food to be dried.

Regardless of the drying method used, a tray with a mesh or slatted bottom is essential. Total surface exposure of food pieces to air flow speeds up the drying process. Free passage of air must occur around the product while it is drying. Trays may be made from an old window screen, a discarded picture frame, or a frame constructed from clean, pitch-free wood strips. Wooden slats or stainless steel, aluminum, or Teflon mesh is used for the tray bottom. Do not use galvanized mesh, because the zinc and cadmium in galvanized screen will give foods a metallic taste, discolor vegetables, and form toxic compounds in acid foods.

In areas where long periods of sunshine are available and time is not a factor, the least expensive drying method is sun drying, using anything from simple improvised trays to solar dryers for exposing the food to the sun's rays. I even met someone who uses the heat build-up in their clunker car for drying food. Where the weather is unreliable, the quantity of food to be dried is large, or where better control of the drying process is desired, the kitchen oven or a small dehydrator is more suitable. Of these methods, the dehydrator is the best choice assuming you have electricity. Dehydrators are equipped with a built-in heat source, a fan, and an air exhaust control; thus, they permit better control of the critical drying factors than the kitchen oven.

DRYING METHODS

Sun Drying

Sun drying is the oldest and least expensive method of drying. All that is needed are some shallow trays and cheese cloth. Air drying performs best in areas where the air is hot (above 85 degrees Fahrenheit), dry (below 60 percent relative humidity), and clean (free of smog and pollutants). Drying periods can be intermittent and variable; therefore, drying times may be prolonged. This method is satisfactory for drying most fruits but is not recommended for vegetables, herbs, meat, or fish.

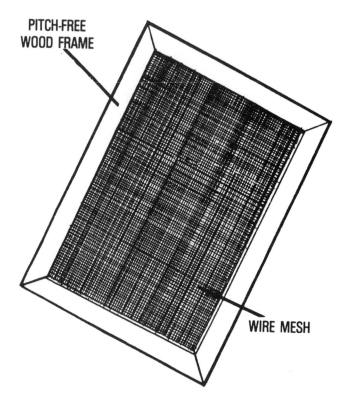

PITCH-FREE WOOD FRAME

WIRE MESH

Drying Tray

Vegetables must be dried under controlled conditions to prevent microbial spoilage. The drying time and temperature are crucial to the tenderness of dried vegetables. Herbs and spices lose aroma, flavor, and color if exposed to direct sun light. The low acidity of meats and fish, combined with low temperature and long drying time, encourages microbial growth and possible spoilage during drying.

Food should first be prepared and pre-treated according to type (See Appendix–Home Drying of Vegetables and Fruit). Spread food pieces one layer deep on trays to allow air to circulate underneath them. Tilting the tray toward the sun will speed up the drying process.

Stir the food two or three times each day so it will dry uniformly. In areas where night-time temperature drops more than 20 degrees or if there is a chance of fog, dew, or rain, bring the trays inside. Drying will probably take three to five days, depending upon type of food, size of food pieces, air temperature, and relative humidity.

Solar Drying

Solar dryers are designed to catch and intensify the heat of the sun under glass or plastic so that the temperature inside the dryer is higher than the outside. They are simple and economical to construct and operate. The dryers resemble and function much like a cold frame for growing plants. Ventilation is an important part of the design. Cool air enters through ventilators at the bottom and as the air heats up, it rises, passes over the food and takes up moisture. The hot, moisture-laden air then escapes through ventilators at the top of the dryer. The solar dryer is recommended in areas where days are dependably sunny, but temperatures and humidities are undesirable for sun drying. They are not as efficient as electric dehydrators, but they do speed up sun drying. Solar dryers also offer more protection from insects, rodents, air pollutants, and rain damage rather than open sun drying.

Prepare the food as recommended for sun drying and spread it one layer deep on the trays. Place the solar dryer where sunlight will fall directly upon the sloping glass or plastic surface for as many hours as possible each day. If convenient, move the dryer two or three times each day to keep the dryer window in direct sunlight. Stir the food two or three times a day so it will dry evenly. When the sun gets low and the dryer interior has cooled, move it inside to prevent moisture pick-up during cool, moist night-time conditions. Drying should be complete in two to three days.

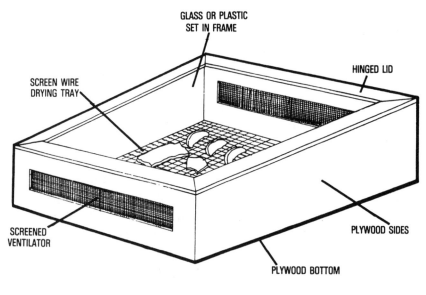

Solar Dryer

Oven Drying

Drying foods in the kitchen oven is a good choice if only a small amount of food is to be dried at one time.

There is little or no investment in equipment; drying can be done anytime during the harvest season regardless of the weather conditions; drying time is continuous and shortened; and most foods can be dried in the oven.

The main disadvantages of oven drying is energy costs and the difficulty in controlling the temperature. Oven drying takes two to three times longer and uses up to twice the amount of energy as drying in a dehydrator. The lowest thermostat setting on older models of gas and electric ovens is too high to dry foods which increases the risk of case hardening and overdrying.

Maintaining a constant low temperature is much easier on newer models. Some newer electric ovens have an exhaust system which circulates air through a venting system. This reduces heat loss and increases drying efficiency. Food dried in an oven will usually be darker, more brittle, and less flavorful than food dried in a dehydrator.

More than one vegetable can be dried at the same time; however, strong-smelling vegetables should be dried separately. Spread one to two pounds of prepared food on each square foot of tray space. The recommended oven load is no more than four to six pounds at a time, distributed over two to four trays.

Preheat the oven to 160 degree Fahrenheit. The temperature will drop 20 degrees when moist food is placed in the oven. Do not use the top element (broiler) of electric ovens. Place the lower oven rack three inches from the bottom of the oven and the other racks above, allowing enough space for two trays to be stacked on each rack.

Trays must be 1 1/2 to two inches narrower than the oven and three inches shorter to permit air circulation. Number the front of each tray to help keep track of the rotation order. Place the trays on the oven racks, alternating one forward and one back (allow about three inches space in back, and three inches space in front, alternately). This arrangement forms a channel which forces the air to flow evenly overall the trays. If more than one tray is placed on a rack, use wood blocks to raise the trays about two inches to allow space for air circulation.

Prop the oven door open at least four inches for the entire drying time to let the moist air out and to maintain a low, even temperature. A fan placed outside the oven and positioned so that air is directed through the opening and across the oven will improve air circulation and reduce drying time. Move the fan from one side to the other occasionally during drying to vary air circulation. Place a thermometer on the top tray with the bulb placed in the back of the oven. Maintain the temperature at 140 degrees Fahrenheit. Vegetables will loose flavor and tenderness if their internal temperature exceeds 140 degrees Fahrenheit.

Check the food often, turning or stirring it occasionally. Reverse the trays every hour (back to front, upper to lower) to assure uniform drying. Watch the temperature carefully. As drying progresses, it will take less heat to maintain the drying temperature. Reduce the temperature when the food is almost dry to prevent overdrying and scorching. Even slight scorching will destroy the flavor and may lower nutritive value.

Dehydrator Drying

Electrically heated, fan equipped food dehydrators are the most efficient means of drying large quantities of foods. Completely assembled dehydrators may be purchased or plans are available for home constructed units.

The heat source in the usual home dehydrator is directly underneath the drying chamber. Therefore, the temperature of the bottom tray is always the hottest and the top tray is always the coolest part in the dehydrator. This factor is important for prevention of scorching and more efficient operation of the dehydrator. Newly manufactured dehydrators feature a horizontal heating airflow system. In this system, air entering from the back is heated as it passes over the heating element and is blown horizontally across the trays. This improves drying efficiency and eliminates the need to rotate trays. See your dehydrator's operators manual for operational details.

Air Drying

This method of drying differs from sun drying since it takes place indoors in a well-ventilated attic, room, or screened-in porch. Herbs, hot peppers, and "leather britches" (whole snap beans air dried on a string) are the most common air dried items, although many people still dry apples, rhubarb, pumpkin and squash rings, corn, and citrus fruit rinds by this method.

Microwave Ovens

Models of microwave ovens currently on the market are not suitable for drying vegetables and fruits. The main disadvantage is the difficulty in maintaining a constant temperature low enough to protect the food from overheating, developing case hardening, or scorching. The energy required to dry the small amounts of food that can be placed in the oven at one time is another disadvantage. Microwave ovens can be used to dry small amount of herbs and spices. The drying time will be short and the food must be carefully watched to prevent overheating and scorching.

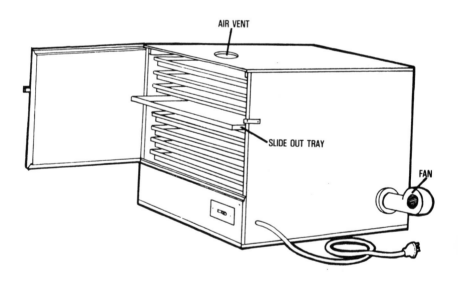

Electric Dehydrator

Dehydrofreezing

This method combines drying with freezing of fruits and vegetables. It is increasing in popularity because fruits preserved this way are as moist as commercially dried fruits and they do not spoil. A major advantage to this method is that the partially dried food take up less than half as much freezer space as fresh frozen foods.

Prepare foods for hydrofreezing the same way as for drying. Dry the fruit or vegetable to about 30 percent of its moisture content. The food should feel moist, soft and pliable, but contain no visible moisture. Remove the food from the drying tray, condition (explained later), package in airtight containers, and freeze. The food must be kept frozen until it is used. Fruits and vegetables preserved this way have good flavor and color, and reconstitute in about one-half the time required for fully dried foods.

PREPARATION OF VEGETABLES FOR DRYING

Select only fresh, tender, high-quality vegetables for drying. If they are not in prime condition for cooking, they are not suitable for drying. They should be prepared and dried on the same day they are harvested.

Wash vegetables in cool water to remove soil and chemical residues. Trim, peel, cut, slice, or shred vegetables according to the directions for each vegetable (discussed later). Remove any fibrous or woody portions and core when necessary, removing all decayed and bruised areas. Keep pieces uniform in size so they will dry at the same rate, and prepare only as many as can be dried at one time. Holding vegetables, even in the refrigerator, after washing and preparation for drying will result in loss of quality and nutrients.

Pretreatment

Blanching is a necessary step in preparing vegetables for drying. It stops the enzyme action which causes loss of color and flavor during drying and storage. It also sets the color and shortens the drying and rehydration time by relaxing the tissue walls so moisture can escape or re-enter more rapidly. By definition blanching is the process of heating vegetables to a temperature high enough to destroy enzymes present in the tissue. In water blanching, the vegetables are submerged in boiling water. In steam blanching, the vegetables are suspended above the boiling water and heated only by the stream. Water blanching usually results in a greater loss of nutrients, but it takes less time than steam blanching.

Water Blanching: Fill a large kettle 2/3 full of water, cover and bring to a rolling boil. Place the vegetables in a wire basket or a colander and submerge them in the water. Cover and blanch according to directions for each vegetable (covered later). If it takes longer than one minute for the water to come back to boiling, too many vegetables were added. Reduce the amount in the next batch.

Steam Blanching: Use a deep kettle with a close fitting lid and a wire basket, colander, or sieve placed so the steam will circulate freely around the vegetables. Place the vegetables loosely in the basket no more than 2

1/2 inches deep. Add several inches of water to the kettle and bring to a rolling boil. Place the basket of vegetables in the kettle. Make sure the water does not come in contact with the vegetables. Cover and steam according to directions for each vegetable (covered later).

After blanching, dip the vegetables in cold water to stop the cooking action, but do not cool them to room temperature. When they feel only slightly hot to the touch, they will be cooled to about 120 degrees Fahrenheit. Drain the vegetables by pouring them directly onto the drying tray held over the sink. Wipe the excess water from underneath the tray and arrange the vegetables in a single layer. Then place the tray immediately in the preheated dehydrator. The heat left in the vegetables from blanching will cause the drying process to begin more quickly.

PREPARATION OF FRUITS FOR DRYING

Preparation

Sort and select the highest quality ripe ready-to-eat fresh fruit. Drying will not improve quality. If fruits are perfect for eating, they are perfect for drying. Handle fruits gently and process them quickly because when they are at the right stage for drying, they are also the most fragile.

Wash all fruits in cold water to remove dirt, insect larvae, and spray residues. Remove all bruised or soft spots and peel, pit, and cut fruits into halves, quarters, or slices. Keep all pieces the same size so they will dry uniformly.

Oxidation and enzyme reactions cause some fruits to turn brown when cut and exposed to air. Unless the fruits are treated to slow these reactions, the browning will continue during drying and storage. Placing the fruit in a solution of sodium bisulfite or ascorbic acid as soon as they are peeled and cut will protect them during preparation. Since holding them in a solution increases the moisture content, do not keep them in the holding solution for more than one hour.

Pretreatment

Apples, apricots, peaches, pears, and nectarines begin to darken as soon as they are cut. They may also lose flavor and vitamins. Pretreating the fruit before drying reduces the discoloration and quality deterioration. Fruit receiving no pre-treatment will be safe to eat, but will be darker in color and lower in quality.

Sulfuring, sulfiting, ascorbic acid, steam blanching, and syrup blanching are all pretreatment methods to keep fruit in prime condition during drying and storage. Each method is described in detail below.

Sulfuring

Sulfuring is the most effective treatment in preventing fruit discoloration. It preserves color, decreases loss of vitamins A and C, and it reduces microbial spoilage and insect infestation.

Outdoors-Sulfur box

Sulfur may be purchased at most drug stores as "flowers of sulfur" or "sublimed sulfur" which usually have a high degree of purity. Garden dusting sulfur is not suitable.

1. Always use sulfur outdoors in the open air. Sulfur fumes can be irritating to the eyes and nose.

2. Use wooden trays with slatted bottoms. Do not use aluminum or galvanized screening materials because sulfur fumes will discolor and corrode most metals.

3. Weigh fruits of the same type and size and spread in a single layer on trays. Place skin side down to help prevent loss of juices.

4. Stack trays at least 1 1/2 inches apart so sulfur fumes can circulate. Raise the bottom tray with wooden blocks or bricks to at least four inches above the ground. Separate trays with small wooden blocks or spools.

5. Pour sulfur about 1/2 inch deep into a clean metal container that is shallow but deep enough to prevent overflow. For each pound of prepared fruit, use one to two teaspoons of sulfur if sulfuring time is less than three hours; three teaspoons if sulfuring time is three hours or longer.

6. Place the container of sulfur beside the stacked trays and ignite. Do not leave burned matches in the container; they may keep the sulfur from burning completely. The burning time of the sulfur will vary with the ventilation, shape of the sulfur container, weather conditions, and the amount of food to be sulfured.

7. Cover the stacked trays with a heavy cardboard carton or a wooden box that has no cracks or openings. The box

should be several inches higher than the stacked trays and at least one to 1 1/2 inches wider around all sides of the trays, including the sulfur placed beside them.

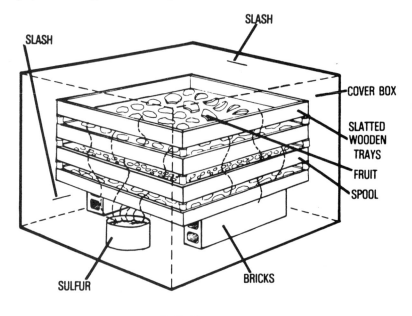

Sulfur Box

8. To provide air for the burning sulfur, leave the bottom of the box slightly propped up, or cut an opening at the bottom about one by six inches, leaving a flap. The opening should be on the side by the sulfur. A slash or small opening may be needed at the upper edge of the opposite side. Lower the box and close the openings after the sulfur has completely burned.

9. Count sulfuring time after the sulfur has finished burning. Various factors affect sulfuring time including fruit texture, size of pieces, and drying method to be used. After sulfuring the recommended length of time

(information to follow), remove the trays and begin drying the fruit.

Indoors - Sodium Sulfite Solution

Sodium sulfite, sodium bisulfite or sodium metabisulfite can be used. Do not use sodium bisulfate. These compounds are available from drug stores or stores that sell wine-making supplies. Be sure to purchase U.S.P. (food grade) or Reagent Grade (pure) sulfur materials. Practical grade is not pure.

Dissolve one to two tablespoons of the sodium sulfite in one gallon of water, and soak the fruit 10-15 minutes. Drain on absorbent towels. Fruit treated in this way will take longer to dry than fruit that is not soaked.

Ascorbic Acid

Pure crystalline ascorbic acid is an antioxidant that helps delay the darkening of certain fruits as they are being prepared for drying. Prepare a solution by dissolving the crystals (2 1/2 teaspoons for apples and one teaspoon for apricots, peaches, nectarines, and pears) in one cup of water. Sprinkle the solution over the fruit pieces, turning them gently until all are coated. One cup of solution will treat about five quarts of cut fruit. Pure ascorbic acid usually can be obtained from most drug stores.

Commercial antioxidant mixtures containing ascorbic acid may be used, but they are not as effective as the pure ascorbic acid. They are available in most drug and grocery stores. Follow label directions when using these preparations.

Steam-Blanching

Fruits may be steam-blanched if they are to be dried under controlled conditions in an oven or dehydrator. Blanching results in a darker colored product than other pretreatment methods and may give a slightly cooked flavor to some fruits such as apricots, peaches, and pears. It may also cause fruits to be soft and somewhat difficult to handle.

Fruits such as grapes, small dark plums, cherries, figs, and some firm berries like blueberries have relatively tough skins with a waxy coating. Removal of the waxy coating and cracking or "checking" the skins on these fruits before drying will reduce the drying time.

To crack the skins, dip fruit into briskly boiling water, then into very cold water, and thoroughly drain on absorbent toweling. The length of the boiling water dip varies from 30-60 or more seconds. The longer dip is necessary for fruit with tough skins, in mature fruit, and for fruit checked at high altitude where the boiling temperature is lower than at sea level.

Syrup-blanching

Syrup-blanching produced a sweetened "candied" type of fruit and helps to retain the color of apples, apricots, figs, nectarines, peaches, pears, and plums.

Make a syrup using one cup corn syrup and one cup sugar to three cups water or use one part corn syrup to one part water. Heat the syrup to boiling, add the prepared fruit, and simmer 10-15 minutes. Remove the

pan from the heat and let the fruit stand in the syrup for
10 minutes longer; then lift out, drain, and cool fruit.

Fruit treated in this way takes longer to dry. It
should be well protected if dried outdoors because it will
be more attractive to insects than non-sweetened fruit.

CONDITIONING

The moisture content of home dried fruit should
be about 15-20 percent. When the fruit is taken from the
dehydrator, the remaining moisture may not be
distributed equally among the pieces because of their size
or their location in the dehydrator. Conditioning or
"sweating" is a process used to equalize the moisture. It
reduces the risk of mold growth and the development of
a candy-like consistency the fruit pieces.

After the dried fruit has cooled, pack it loosely in
plastic or glass jars. Seal the containers and let them
stand for 7 to 10 days. The excess moisture in some
pieces will be absorbed by the drier pieces. Shake the jars
daily to separate the pieces and check for moisture
condensation. If condensation develops in the jar, return
the fruit to the dehydrator for more drying.

Home dried vegetables should have a moisture
content of four to five percent. Because they are dried to
such a waterless state, they do not need to be conditioned.

PASTEURIZING

Some foods need to be pasteurized after drying to
prevent insect spoilage during storage. Preparation and
drying of foods does not always remove or destroy insect

larvae or eggs that may be on them. Also, insects may contaminate the food during drying. If the insect larvae or eggs are not destroyed before the food is packaged, they will continue to grow and spoil the food.

Two methods are recommended for pasteurizing dried foods. Either one destroys insects and their eggs.

Freezer Method: Seal the food in heavy plastic bags. Place the bags in a freezer set at 0 degrees Fahrenheit or below and leave them for two to four days before storing.

Oven Method: Place the food on a tray or in a shallow pan, and put in an over preheated to 150 degree Fahrenheit for 30 minutes. Package the food as soon as it is cool.

PACKAGING AND STORING

Dried foods are immediately susceptible to insect contamination and moisture reabsorption and should be packaged as soon as they are cool. Pack foods as tightly as possible without crushing into clean, dry, insect-proof containers.

Glass jars, metal can, or moisture and vapor proof freezer cartons make good containers for storing dried foods. Heavy duty plastic bags are acceptable, but are not insect and rodent proof.

Pack food in amounts that can be used within several days after the package has been opened. Everytime a package is opened the food is exposed to air and moisture and loses quality.

Fruit that has been sulfured should not touch metal. Place the fruit in a plastic bag before storing it in a metal can. Sulfur fumes will react with the metal and cause color changes in the fruit.

To protect the food from insects and to prevent reabsorption of moisture, lids should be sealed to the containers. Wrap the rim edge with a plasticized pressure sensitive tape or with a clean one inch strip of cloth that is still warm after being dipped in paraffin.

Dried foods should be stored in cool, dry, dark areas. Recommended storage times for dried food range from four months to one year. Because food quality is affected by heat, the storage temperature helps determine the length of storage; the higher the temperature, the shorter the storage time. For best quality and maximum storage, the temperature should not exceed 60 degrees Fahrenheit.

Foods that are packaged seemingly "bone dry" can spoil if moisture is reabsorbed during storage. Check dried foods frequently during storage to see if they are still dry. Glass containers are excellent for storage because any moisture that collects on the inside can be seen easily. Foods affected by moisture, but not spoiled, should be used immediately or reheated and repackaged. Moldy foods should be discarded.

PREPARING DRIED FOODS FOR TABLE USE

Using dried foods for cooking is simple. You just replace the water removed by the drying process. All dried vegetables except leafy vegetables and tomatoes should be placed in water and rehydrated before cooking. Place one cup of dried vegetables in 1 1/2 to two cups of water and soak until they reabsorb most of the water lost in drying. Warm water will shorten the rehydration time, but cold water may be used. Rehydrating takes 20 minutes to two hours, depending on the vegetable, the thickness of the pieces, and the water temperature. Refrigerate the vegetables if the soaking time is more than two hours. Microorganism growth can occur and cause spoilage of the rehydrated vegetables stored at room temperature.

To cook, bring vegetables to a boil and simmer until they are tender. Leafy vegetables, cabbage, and tomatoes do not need to be soaked. Add sufficient water to keep them covered and simmer until tender.

Like fresh vegetables, dried ones will lose both texture and flavor if overcooked. Since vegetables are already partially cooked, they can be prepared for table use in a short time. Allow excess water to evaporate during cooking or use the stock for part of the water needed in other recipes.

Many vegetables lose their fresh flavor, color, and overall eye appeal during drying and are usually not used as side dishes for this reason. They are best used as ingredients in the preparation of combination dishes such as soups, stews, or casseroles. The addition of herbs or spices such as basil, garlic, onion, or chili sauce during cooking improves the flavor.

Dried vegetables can be flaked or powdered and used as seasonings in soups or sauces, or sprinkled over salads. The vegetables can be blended separately or several vegetables can be blended together. The vegetables should be very dry and brittle for flaking. Place pieces of vegetables in a blender and blend until the desired size is obtained. Place chopped vegetables in air tight containers and store them in a cool dry area. The storage life for flakes and powders is about one month.

Fruit requires from one to eight hours to reconstitute. The time varies with the kind of fruit, the size of pieces and the temperature of the soak water. Oversoaking produces a loss of flavor and sometimes a mushy water-logged texture. Fermentation spoilage occurs if fruit is soaked too long. Drying does not kill the bacteria, yeasts, and molds on the fruit. Refrigerate the fruit if the soaking time is more than one hour.

To cook reconstituted fruit, cover and simmer in the soak water to retain the nutritive quality.

Less sugar may be required when cooking dried fruit than when cooking fresh fruit. During the drying process, some of the starch in the fruit may change to sugar. When sugar is used, it should be added at the end of the cooking process so it will not interfere with the fruit's absorption of water.

Adding a few grains of salt helps to bring out the natural sweetness of most fruits. Lemon, orange or grapefruit juice added to the fruit just before serving will help give it a fresh fruit flavor and add vitamin C.

NUTRITIONAL VALUE OF DRIED FOODS

The nutritional value of dried foods, not unlike that of foods preserved by canning and freezing, depends largely on the care exercised in preparation, processing, and storage. Generally, the nutrient content of dried foods compares favorably with that of food preserved by other methods. Some of the sugars, salt, and water-soluble vitamins are lost during preparation. Some of the volatile oils and ester and readily oxidizable substances like ascorbic acid (vitamin C) are lost during the drying process. The vitamin A content of vegetables decreases during storage. The loss of vitamin A is greatest in unblanched vegetables. Carbohydrates, minerals, and proteins are concentrated but are otherwise unaffected by drying. Further loss of nutrients can occur during storage unless the foods are properly packaged and stored.

To keep the nutritional losses to a minimum, package dried foods in airtight containers, store them at the lowest temperature possible, and consume them within several months to one year after processing.

See Appendix for additional information on Home Drying of Vegetables and Fruits.

CHAPTER VI

Rabbits: A Proven Urban Meat Source You Can Raise Anywhere

Rabbits make an excellent survival food source. Rabbits are very efficient producers, and the cost of their feed versus the amount of meat they produce is minimal. In addition, they require little space, shelter, and labor. The amount of protein in rabbit meat is high, approaching that of chicken and beef. The leanness of the meat and the resulting low calories, however, while being an asset in most normal diets, may be the only fault of rabbit as an ideal food for emergency situations. When shortage of food may make calories for energy a prime concern, one cannot depend upon rabbits alone for energy.

Production of rabbits is unique in that it can be kept a secret. One can raise rabbits almost anywhere without anyone else knowing. My area has zoning laws that prohibit goats, chickens, etc.; but there is nothing specified about rabbits. Rabbits make no noise, and when the manure is removed regularly, they do not create offensive odors. I have raised rabbits with good result in wire cages in a corner of my garage. The manure is rich fertilizer for the garden, and it also makes an excellent worm bed.

Rabbits are very prolific, hardy, and less disease-prone than other meat-producing animals. They may produce young thirty days after breeding and can raise seven or more little rabbits from each litter, four or five times a year. The net result is that one doe (female) can produce thirty to forty rabbit fryers each year. These fryers will dress out at 2 to 3 pounds each in about eight weeks.

Using rabbits for survival purposes is not new. I recall talking once with a woman who lived in Europe during the German blockade. She told me her town experienced such food deprivation that the population ate all the leaves off the trees. Yet she was fortunate to have rabbits which became the difference between her own life and death by starvation, and the rabbit meat was also useful for bartering.

Rabbits can be used for more than food. Extra income can come from sales to the public for pets and to laboratories for research. These concerns should help determine production plans; therefore, one considering going into rabbit farming might make a preliminary check with research centers and pet shops to determine their interest in sizes and breeds.

BREEDS

Commercially bred rabbits should not be confused with pet rabbits. Rabbits bred for meat grow larger, develop faster, produce meat quicker, and resist most diseases. For meat production, three of the established breeds are the Californian, New Zealand White and Checkered Giant. A mature doe of these breeds grows to 9-11 pounds.

In an urban environment it is sometimes difficult to find sources of good rabbits, but most rural areas have annual agricultural fairs that have rabbits exhibited. The local county extension agent can provide advice. He can also provide references and addresses of farmers' bulletins published in the area which will list farm-related items for sale.

Outdoor wood/wire cages are economical and easy to construct.

One should start rabbit production with just a buck and a couple of does. Firsthand experience with a small start can provide guidance in making decisions about expansion. Without a good knowledge of breeding stock, one will have to rely on a recommended producer of rabbits for the initial stock. Always to be rejected is any animal that looks sick; has diarrhea, a runny nose, or a cough; or does not seem bright and alert. Usually a rabbit that acts lively and appears curious and friendly is a good choice. Normally, the friendlier the doe, the better mother she will become and the easier to handle. The buck should have well descended testicles that are not shrunken or dry. Most bucks and does can be counted on to produce well for nearly three years.

HOUSING

Rabbits can be raised all year. Whereas many fear for a rabbit's weathering the winter, in actuality heat may be the primary problem. Heat can be a deadly enemy, so in hot climates, some shading is necessary–the rabbits must be able to choose to be in the shade. In the extreme North, to protect from the cold wind, plastic or wood panels should be attached to the sides and rear of the cage from the roof line to the ground. Openings here should face to the south and east. During strong, icy winds, an old sheet or table cloth can be draped over the front of the pen.

I make my cages extra roomy so the rabbits will not be crowded. I even have a hinged door between adjoining cages that I open to allow for additional movement when my rabbit count is low. Larger breeds need pens no smaller than 2 1/2 feet wide, 5-6 feet long, and 2 feet tall. The door openings should be large enough to allow the breeder easy access for cleaning the interior and for adding nest boxes as needed. The floors should

Indoor cages protect rabbits from the elements.

be made of 1/2 inch hardware cloth or 12-gauge galvanized wire mesh. The hardware cloth has a tendency to sag unless supported by cross members from

underneath. If all-wire cages are used, bending most of
the wire sides and bottom removes the need for wood
framing. To bind the fabricated wire cage wall together,
use "pig ear" tag clips which can be purchased from
farmer's supply stores. I prefer all-wire cages because
they are light and easy to clean. Also they can be
suspended from the ceiling or under shelves.

A well designed cage uses a hinged roof for access.

Rabbits are social creatures. Since they do not like to be alone, cages should be arranged to allow a pair to stay next to each other.

Rabbits will always use the same corner of the cage for their excretion. It will usually be a back corner. If the cage is placed near a wall, the wall will get sprayed, thus strong odors may result. To avoid such offensive odors, the cage can be hung away from the wall, or the wall lined with metal roof flashing to be hosed down regularly.

DISEASE AND INJURY

Cleanliness of the cage, food, and water containers is the best disease preventative for rabbits. Any that are not acting normal should be isolated for several weeks. Newly acquired rabbits should be routinely isolated for several weeks as a precautionary measure. There are few effective treatments for diseases affecting rabbits, thus most owners destroy any sick ones.

Most physical injuries of rabbits are caused by improper handling. When picked up, a rabbit will kick and scratch and likely cause a novice handler to drop it and inadvertently cause the animal injury. The best method to pick up a rabbit is to grasp and lift it by the fold of skin over its shoulder with one hand, then with the other hand, support its rump. If the rabbit struggles, it can be pinned under the arm. A baby rabbit can be grasped also in the loin area and picked up.

A rabbit's toenails need to be clipped. They can grow needle sharp. If the foot is held near the light, the inner cone of the toenail can be seen. The nails should be cut with a regular fingernail clipper just short of the tip of the cone. A toe nail will bleed if it is cut too short.

FEEDING AND WATERING

The best feed dispensers are those available from a farmers' supply. They will hold several days' provision of rabbit feed and will prevent fouling from the rabbits' excretion. I began with a feed dispenser that mounted to the exterior of my cage. I was keeping the pens under a large shelf in my barn where, before long, the largest of my "children"–Totsie, my horse–discovered the feed dispenser. She would nudge it until it fell to the ground. I now use, instead, a heavy crockery dog dish inside the cage. Its weight keeps it from turning over. However, the commercial feed dispenser is better when the young are around because they will soil both the food and water if they can get into the dishes.

Rabbits are vegetarians, but they need protein. Rabbit producers normally use a commercial pelletized ration that is designed for rabbits. The ration should include salt and pressed alfalfa. Too much garden greens can be harmful and cause diarrhea. Diets should never be changed rapidly, especially for a pregnant doe, because she may resist the new feed and stop eating.

As a supplement, legume hays such as alfalfa, clover, and vetch offer good protein but are not necessary sources. I prune tree branches and give them to my rabbits to debark and gnaw on. I also drop in grass, carrots, and garden leftovers such as beets and turnips. These root crops are good for winter use due to a shortage of green vegetables during that time of the year. Oats, wheat, barley, etc., and soft varieties of corn can be fed whole or in milled form. Dry bread can also be used to add variety. When commercial feed was in short supply for me, I utilized more twigs, grass, etc., as close to a natural diet as possible, while supplementing with commercial feed and small salt blocks, depending upon their availability.

Pigeons and rabbits are successfully raised together.

Since rabbits are nocturnal, I feed them in the evening. Tasty garden produce should be saved as dessert after the commercial feed.

Fortunately, winter weather does not necessitate additional food requirements. A mature rabbit will eat around six to eight ounces a day, and overfeeding can reduce or stop production. A shiny coat and a lack of thinness or fatness are good signs of health and proper feeding.

I use the same type ceramic crock for water as I do for food. It is heavy and, due to its sloping insides, will not crack when the water freezes. A small outdoor water heater can be used to stop freezing if a power source is available, but one must be careful with the placement of the power cord, for rabbits will chew it. Sometimes during the summer I use a commercial quart plastic bottle with a ballpoint type nozzle, but I have to be watchful because a rabbit can chew the plastic cap through the wire. Watering dishes must be kept clean (a bleach solution can be used periodically to disinfect them) and the water changed daily as a preventative against liver coccidiosis. A rabbit with a litter can drink a gallon of water a day, so adequate provision of water must be made. A fresh water supply near the cages is helpful.

NEST BOXES

When a doe kindles (is near delivery), she will need a nesting box and straw to build her nest. A good nest box can be made from anything that will provide seclusion for the doe and protection of the litter. It should provide access for the young to move in and out as they explore the pen. Good ventilation and drainage in the ends and bottom of the box can be allowed by drilling 1/4 inch holes. This is important because in cold weather, urine or water collection can cause the young to freeze to the bottom. The basic dimensions of a nest box should be one foot wide, two feet long and one foot tall. One end of the box should be open to allow entry with a lip board six inches high to contain the new babies. To reduce gnawing, the wood corners can be covered with metal strips that are used to edge carpets. If the box has a flat top, the mother will enjoy sitting on the top to escape the young as they get older. A nail keg obtained from the hardware store will make a good nest box if one-fourth of the open end is covered with a board. The board can be extended past the edge to stabilize the round keg.

In the winter, I line the sides and top of each box with cardboard and stuff it with hay. The doe will burrow inside the straw and use the hair from her neck to make the nest.

Nest boxes should be kept clean and should be disinfected between each use. A farmer's supply store is a good source for disinfectant. To complete sterilization, a fire from a rolled newspaper torch or a propane torch can be used to singe and remove remaining hairs. An afternoon in the sun will also help sanitize the box.

BREEDING

From the time of weaning, the sexes should be kept separate except for breeding. Determining the sex of a rabbit is difficult until one has experience in doing or seeing it done. For younger rabbits, one squeezes the sides of the sex organ with the fingers. A doe's genitals looks like a very small slit and the buck's genitals will look circular and have a protrusion.

Cages made from welded wire and wire clips are easy to clean and maintain.

The correct age for mating varies. Medium breeds are ready around six months and larger breeds nearer nine months. A doe should be mated as soon as she reaches maturity. A doe will give visible signs when she is ready to mate. She will be nervous and restless. She will gather near other rabbits in the next cage and will rub her chin on parts of the cage and other objects in it. It is best to take her to the buck's pen. Mating will occur in a matter of minutes; afterwards,the doe should be transferred back to her pen. The process should be repeated in four hours to insure impregnation.

Generally one buck can be used to breed ten does, serving several times a week. Many owners like to keep accurate records of the breeding process including names of buck and doe, breeding date, date of births, number in litter, and number of survivors from each litter.

The gestation period for rabbits is about a month, and the nursing period around eight weeks. A doe can be mated six weeks after a litter's birth. If a litter is lost at birth, there can be a shorter wait before she is bred again.

If mating is delayed too long, breeding difficulties occur. I recall my original experience of raising "survival" rabbits. Not prone to slaughter animals unless the food stores are shut down, I intended to raise only a few rabbits in order to learn the basics and planned to begin my breeding-and-slaughtering-phase whenever need occurred. Unfortunately, a year later I found that if a doe is not bred in "her" proper time, she becomes barren.

PREGNANCY

Rabbits can have false pregnancy. Two weeks after mating, the doe can be checked for pregnancy. Without using much pressure, one should feel the doe's abdomen in front of the pelvis, moving the thumb gently back and forth on one side and the forefingers on the other side. If the doe is pregnant, marble-sized lumps can be felt. If not, she may be placed with the buck again in another week. Then, if she is not pregnant, mating her again can be attempted in 31 days.

KINDLING

The time between mating and kindling (birthing) averages thirty-one days. On the 25th day, the kindlebox should be placed into the pen. Providing the doe extra greens now may be beneficial. Several days before birthing, she will gather straw and pull hair from her chest to make her nest. The delivery will normally take place at night. If the litter is born outside the box, or if part of the litter is elsewhere, all the litter must be moved into the box because a doe will not gather up nor nurse the separated young. Activity around the cage should be reduced. Caution must be exercised in checking the babies because an excited doe may kill the new ones. One should tempt the doe to the other side of the cage with a treat while checking them. Rubbing a nervous doe's nose with Vaseline will reduce her ability to smell human odor on the babies. If the doe seems too nervous after kindling, she should be left alone. The babies can be checked and any dead ones removed the next day.

If, in the winter, the doe has not pulled enough hair to insulate the young, the task must be completed for her to insure a warm nest. Some breeders save extra hair from other rabbits for this purpose. On the other hand, in an area of hot summer months, breeding during the heat should be avoided. A litter may not survive in a hot, fur-insulated nest.

Babies will open their eyes in about two weeks. At about twenty days, the little rabbits will emerge from the nest. They are weaned by eight weeks and are ready then for butchering if that is desired.

BUTCHERING

Rabbits are relatively easy to butcher. There are two basic methods of killing a rabbit. One is by stunning it with a blow on the head just in front of the ears. The second method is to hold the rabbit by the hind legs with one hand while using the other hand to jerk the head downward. The fingers of the jerking hand are placed under the rabbit's jaw with the thumb on the rabbit's neck quickly pressing and bending it backwards. The rapid dislocation of the neck renders the animal instantly unconscious.

Butchering must be carried out in a clean area. To begin, one pierces the tendon above the hock on a single hind leg with a hook made from a bent piece of metal. The body is hung by this tendon and the head cut off. The carcass is allowed to hang and bleed until the dripping stops. Next, the other three feet and tail are cut off. Then the butcher makes a cut down on the inside of the two hind legs and across the groin area to peal off the skin. It will pull off rather easily. Next, he guts the carcass after making a shallow cut in the stomach just large enough to allow guiding a knife with his finger so as to avoid cutting the intestines. Lastly, the entrails are removed. If the liver is spotted, it must be thrown away, as coccidiosis is indicated. (Coccidiosis will not harm the meat but suggests that other rabbits need treatment. A vet should be consulted.) The carcass is washed in cold water to remove blood and hair. Then it is refrigerated.

Rabbit being held prior to dislocation of neck.

As in any survival undertaking, firsthand experience is invaluable to insure effectiveness. To get started, I made a wire cage and obtained two rabbits. The knowledge gained from that beginning could not have been acquired any other way. I now know that most of my mistakes are behind me and, because of my practical learning, I am capable of being an effective rabbit producer in record set-up time.

CHAPTER VII

Pigeons: An Unusual Urban Meat Source

Desperate times lead to extreme measures. During the course of an oppressive Paris winter, author Ernest Hemingway discovered that the threat of starvation could bring unusual food to the table.

In order to feed his family, he resorted to catching pigeons in the Luxembourg Gardens when the gendarme went off duty. Having lured the pigeons with a handful of corn, Hemingway would capture the creatures. He then concealed the birds in his son's baby carriage and left quickly without being seen.

Pigeon-raising offers an excellent alternate food source with a minimum time or expense even to many who have limited space. Wild pigeons are not as tasty as specially bred pigeons, but they cost nothing and take care of themselves. I enjoy the aspects of raising pigeons as a hobby, knowing that in a time of need, I can have an available food source. When capturing and raising wild pigeons, I can have a meat source that would be able to take care of themselves should I become financially unable to feed them.

Thousands of people in this country breed pigeons and train them for races because they enjoy the competition of that sport. Some manage squab farms as commercial food enterprises. Others, like myself, raise them for a hobby and as a potential food source. I became interested in pigeon-raising when I visited a friend who has a large flock. It was there I first found pigeons fascinating to watch as they fly from the loft and soar into the sky. The rush of their wings is exhilarating as they leave and also when, after about twenty minutes, they begin singly and majestically returning to their loft so all are soon back home.

Pigeon raising offers a hobby that can not only pay for itself by providing meat for one's own table, but it can also provide a good secondary income. I heard of one farmer who began a successful squab farm by first trapping wild pigeons and transplanting them to his facilities. Before long, the wild birds were setting up house. When they began to lay, their eggs were replaced with commercially bred ones. The new parents raised the squabs with their own foraging efforts. When the squabs were ready to sell, there had been no cost involved except that of the initial eggs.

In a survival situation, you may not be able to go out and buy a special breed of pigeon that you desire. In this case, several wild pigeons can be trapped and trained to adopt your loft as their home. For example, if a wild pigeon is restrained in the loft with a cage over his exit that allows a view of the outside surroundings, within several weeks he will adapt to his new home. Some owners clip the tips of one wing so flight is difficult. This insures that escape is difficult during the initial tests of freedom when the cage is removed. If all goes well, the captured wild pigeons will return to the loft and begin to nest.

The difference between rural pigeons and city pigeons is their diet. The country birds gather food from the seed-producing countryside; city pigeons feed on the handouts and litter of people. They thrive on sloppy city-keeping; garbage cans left open and spilling over; the crumbs of discarded crusts and scraps. When using a recently trapped city pigeon for food, I would prefer to fatten him up with proper food in clean conditions.

This structure is used on windless days for an exercise area.

FACILITIES

The first "specific" to be considered in pigeon-raising is the facility–or pigeon loft. Normally any shelter will provide a home for pigeons. Yet usually the flock will grow larger than one expects, thus making necessary a decision concerning disposal of the excess birds or expansion of the provided space.

Whatever structure is used, it should be well ventilated but not drafty. The pigeons will need access to sunlight and will withstand cold that is not extreme. Dry quarters are important. A pigeon loft can be an old building, barn, chicken house, storage building or an attic. A wire cage can be attached on the outside over the openings in the wall to allow the pigeons to see their surroundings while having access to a roost on the inside.

ENEMIES

In an area that has hawks, one should try to use a loft away from trees. One pigeon hobbyist lost several of his favorites to a local hawk that would wait in a nearby tree for the right moment then swoop down and pluck pigeons off the loft roof. Where the hawks have moved out of an urban situation, such would not be a problem. In Georgia, hawks seem to concentrate here during the winter. During this period, my pigeons are not allowed to fly. A large local wild pigeon population is a good sign that there are no hawks in the area.

Many areas are overrun with feral cats. Once tame cats, or kittens from tame cats, go wild, they are well able to provide for themselves. They eat chiefly rodents, but enjoy birds too. When a cat gets into a pigeon loft, if it knows it can get out, it may kill many pigeons. Cats are easy to trap. Nearly every cat will go to a fish bait and if you use a box trap or a catch-alive device, fish for bait will draw them in.

A simple outdoor feeder is used for wild pigeons.

The Norwegian rat may be the greatest mammalian enemy of pigeons. They can chew their way in and kill at random. They will even enter in the daytime. If you are in a situation where commercial rat poison is not available, you can try dog food. Dog food left out for several meals will lure a rat into dropping its guard. Then set the bait in your trap or mix Warfarin in the food. Warfarin reacts within four days. It is safer than most rat poisons because one meal of it will not kill a pigeon or pet.

Raccoons have destroyed many lofts. They prowl at night and are exceedingly adept climbers. They are also easy to trap when baited with fish.

Opossums prowl at night. They are excellent climbers and can get into any loft through holes even smaller than pigeons can enter. They will seemingly kill for the joy of killing. Kill every opossum you catch in or around your coop. If liberated, it will try to enter again.

Snakes can enter a loft through coarse wire screening and eat pigeon eggs. The remedy, of course, consists in screening with finer-mesh wire.

PIGEON LOFTS

A couple I met began raising several pigeons for the fun of it in a small utility building with a split door. The building was used for their rabbits as well as the pigeons. The lower part of the door was kept shut to keep the rabbits in while the upper section was left open to allow the pigeons access to the outdoors. The upper section was never closed except for evening or during severe cold spells. The pigeons came and went as they pleased. Most of the time they stayed either on the roof of the storage building sunning themselves or inside on their nests. Before long the flock grew–not only from

Pigeons make themselves at home on top of their cages.

reproduction. Wild pigeons in the area realized there was good lodging to be had, and they joined the domestic birds in the loft. Fortunately the owners had not experienced any problems from the wild pigeons harboring and transmitting diseases to the domestic birds. Unfortunately, both pigeons and poultry can transmit diseases to each other. Clean living conditions and disease free birds remove most problems.

A simple backyard storage building serves as a pigeon loft.

The type of building and size of the loft can vary. To begin with, each pigeon needs a floor space of 1 1/2 square feet. Most pigeon-raisers attach a flight pen for exercise and access to sunshine. I prefer to let my pigeons out daily, allowing them to do most of their own exercising while foraging for themselves. To make a flight pen, wire mesh is used with openings no larger than one inch which will not allow sparrows and other birds to enter, for they can carry mites and disease. Closeable windows allow the pigeons access back and forth to the loft and the flight pen. The windows can be shut on extreme weather days.

CARE: CLEANLINESS

Keeping the pigeon quarters clean is very important to reduce insect pests and diseases. Several times a year, the pigeons should be removed to another area and the loft cleaned and sprayed with an insecticide. Fresh painting is also a good idea. Having made these recommendations, I must also state that I know many small flock owners who do very little cleaning. They put sawdust on the floor to catch droppings and sometimes blow out the loft. Others use a wire mesh floor and collect the droppings from the ground below to use as fertilizer.

All bird manure, including chicken manure, affords a splendid medium for the growth of fungus organisms. When the manure dries and becomes dust, it can, if inhaled, produce a human disease called Cryptococcosis. In reality, very few cases have been reported. Dust from pigeon manure can also cause "Pigeon Keeper's Disease." It causes pneumonia-like symptoms and is very rare. Raising pigeons like any agricultural project requires basic cleanliness.

Pigeons like to keep themselves clean. A shallow, flat crockery dish makes a good pigeonbath. Accessible bathing water is especially important during nesting. The moisture from the bathing is carried back to the nest and will assist in keeping the eggshells soft (a soft eggshell helps in hatching). Bathing water should be provided three or more times a week. It should be removed, also, regularly, after bathing is completed, so the pigeons will not drink it.

SELECTION: BREEDS

Pigeons are divided into three main types: fancy, flyer, and utility. From a survival standpoint, the utility pigeons are best. They grow into a large size and have white skin. In addition, they are highly productive, hatching up to 11 pairs of squabs a year. Within the utility class, there are many sub-breeds. I am most familiar with the popular King pigeon. It is bred in many colors, and the squabs are in demand by fine restaurants. The King is a medium-sized pigeon with a stout, chunky build and an adult weight reaching 35 ounces. Tame and prolific, the King produces white-skinned squabs in the one-pound range.

SEX

When purchasing pigeons, it is important to distinguish between the sexes. To do this is difficult until the birds are several months old. The shape and behavior of a pigeon provide clues to determining its sex. As a general rule, the male has a thicker neck and is larger than a female. Also, the male tends to display periods of cooing and dancing in which he performs complete turns. The female will coo regularly but not to the extent nor performance of the male. Seeing two birds cooperate in making a nest does not mean that these pigeons are a heterosexual pair. Any two pigeons confined together will make a nest, but, of course, only a mixed pair can produce eggs.

An experienced breeder holds one of his "special" birds.

Normally pigeons mate for life but when separated, they will accept a different mate. It is best to keep mated pairs together; otherwise, the "free" pigeons will try to entice other pigeon's mates.

A professionally constructed loft designed for easy maintenance.

Both the male and female will assist in the nest building, the incubating process, and the care of the young. Normally the female builds the nest while the male gathers the material. Then the female will spend the majority of the time incubating the eggs with the male's periodic help in nestsitting.

NEST BOXES

A one-cubic foot area is adequate for nesting purposes. An open-front shelf arrangement with vertical dividers works well using 1"x12" shelving boards. Fortunately, a pigeon is very creative and will find some make-shift arrangement if a nesting box is not provided. In the case mentioned before where pigeons were raised in a rabbit hutch, some of the pigeons made nests on top of the rabbit cages. Extra nesting boxes should be provided in addition to one for each pair of pigeons in the flock. It is best to provide two nesting boxes for each pair. Often pigeons will lay and start incubating a second clutch of eggs before their squabs are fully grown.

Pigeon nests are crudely constructed and sometimes consist of a small, wallowed-out pile of straw. If pigeons do not have access to the outside, nesting material such as grass straw and pine needles must be provided.

A mother pigeon lays two eggs, each weighing half an ounce or more. After about 17 days, the eggs hatch. Within two to three weeks after hatching, the young may weigh more than the parents and be ready for harvesting. It is at this stage in development, when they are helpless because they cannot yet fly and are the fattest and most tender, that they are a gourmet's delight. Older birds can be harvested at night because they will not try to fly in the dark.

Using cedar sawdust or chips in the bottom of the nest boxes may reduce problems from mites. Additionally, one may want to sprinkle a little mite powder into the nests to prevent insect pest infestations, especially when wild pigeons are involved.

PERCHES

Within the loft, pigeons need a place to perch. A perch made from 2"x2" boards works well. Perches should not be placed under each other or they will be fouled by pigeons roosting above. Perches at eye level or below become an aid in catching pigeons. (Tame pigeons can be easily caught but wild pigeons may need to be taken from their perch at night.)

FEEDS

There are several good commercially mixed feeds available on the market. Pet stores and farmer's supply stores are good sources. Those who allow their birds access to the outside can use cracked corn as a supplement and allow the birds to forage for everything else on their own. A good commercial feed will nurture healthy pigeons; but we have all seen how well a wild flock of pigeons survives in the city from whatever they can find to eat.

With just a few birds, one may prefer to feed by hand twice a day. The provision can be placed in a feed dish or spread on the ground or the floor of the loft. If the feed is not taken in 30 minutes, the amount of the leftover should be reduced from the next batch. It is better to underfeed than to overfeed. A feeder used for poultry will work well to keep the pigeons from fouling their feed.

Pigeons enjoy a "flight run" for sun and exercise.

WATER

Pigeons need clean drinking water at all times, and provisions should be made to keep it from freezing in the winter. I use a poultry watering device that has a heater. Additionally, the bath water must be kept separate from the drinking water.

GRIT

Pigeons, like other fowl, need grit for digestion. Available from the same sources as the feed, commercial grit contains crushed rock and minerals in a combination to provide for strong eggshells and general health of the birds. Grit should be available to the birds at all times, due to the mineral additives, even if the pigeons are allowed access to the outside.

CONCLUSION

There are very few meat sources that will proliferate at the rate of pigeons or are as self-sustaining as they. In a time of need, wild pigeons can provide food in most urban as well as rural settings.

A good source of pigeons and supplies may be found from the following suppliers:

Global Pigeon Supplies (Supplies) - 2301-B Rowland Avenue. Savannah, GA 31404 (912) 356-1320.

Carol Elmore (Live Squab) - 129 Laverne St. Sumter, SC 29153 (803) 773-8181.

Robert Cash (Show Kings) - 1378 Sweet Shrub Dr. S.W. Eatonton, GA 31024 (706) 485-8854. Ask for culls.

CHAPTER VIII

HOW TO USE FISH TRAPS

FISH TRAPS

Traps are useful for catching fish and more effective than single line fishing. They force the fish to enter through a funnel where it is difficult to find their way out. Fish traps operate unattended and are very effective. They are best used in specific locations for a period of time. Depending on which trap one builds, they can be very labor intensive to construct and not portable. Obviously, most traps should be constructed in advance while materials are available. On the other hand willow traps are not limited by manmade materials.

Let me warn you, this type of fishing is illegal in many states and should only be undertaken in a survival situation. Although some states allow specific type traps to be used with a commercial fishing license. In Georgia, using traps in private lakes is legal. Be sure to check with your local state fish and game authorities. One survivalist I know always has fish. He places traps in public lakes after dark so no one will see where the traps are and what he is doing. He collects the catch at night.

When making a trap, be sure to put in an access trap door to remove the catch and for changing the bait. It can be held in place with an innertube rubber strip. If chicken wire is used, use a heavier wire perimeter to stiffen both the opening and the door.

In Macon, Georgia while on a flooding assignment, I tested my first homemade trap. It was round, constructed of chicken wire, with heavy wire circles spaced along the length of the trap for reinforcement. I baited it with a can of dog food and set the trap where a small creek entered the Ocmulgee river. Laying in bed that night thinking about the prospects of a large catch, I realized I forgot to latch the trap's door. The second day I corrected my oversight, reset the trap but cut both my hands on a piece of protruding wire. That night there was a heavy rain that washed the trap under a log. It took an hour to untangle. I learned to use a heavier retrieval line. The next day I had a four pound carp in the trap, then there was nothing for two days. I changed bait to a container of chicken livers and caught a three pound catfish. Excited about my catch, I placed the trap and fish back in the water so I could bring a friend to show off my catch only to find the fish had escaped through a gap in my poorly constructed trap door. Then nothing for two days. Next I moved the trap and caught two turtles that had drowned because they could not reach the surface for air after they were trapped. Then came a storm with rising waters that nearly washed away my tie-off point. When the waters resided, I almost could not retrieve the trap because it weighed fifty pounds and was full of leaves. It appeared the trap funnel had turned upstream and directed the soaked leaves into the trap. So it went, each day I learned more about how to use a trap. Looking back, it seemed like such a simple task. But like all skills, it takes practice to be proficient.

Trapping fish is not a panacea for finding food. For example, baited traps normally catch roughage fish such as catfish, carp and buffalo. Unbaited traps with side wings will direct all types of feeding fish into a trap. Unfortunately, catfish are more difficult to catch during

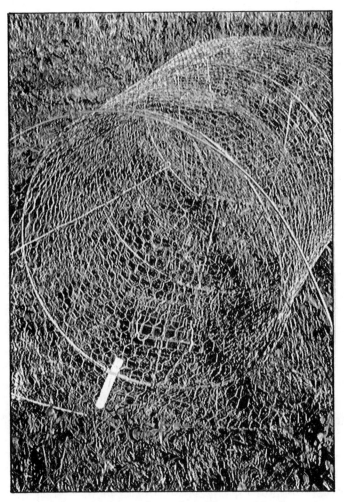

Commercially made traps can be purchased from rural hardware stores.

the cold months when they almost stop eating and go into hibernation. Also, rigid wire traps are difficult to transport and will quickly rust unless coated with a tar substance. Netted hoop traps that collapse provide ease of transportation.

My initial efforts to catch a few fish were quickly over-shadowed while on disaster duty in Dothan, Alabama. There I met a commercial catfish fisherman who fished Walter George Reservoir and the Chattahoochee river. He baits his traps with old molded cheese and checks his traps every three days. On each recovery of a trap, he regularly catches 100 pounds of catfish.

TRAP BAITS

As mentioned earlier, baited traps normally catch only roughage fish. Usually the bait used for traps is the by-product left from gutting other fish. A bait such as cut fish can be tied in the tail of the trap (opposite the opening). For catfish bait, try sour corn (fresh or dry) let soak and sour. Put in nylon stocking. With soybean meal, mix 2 buckets of water and 50 pounds of meal. Soak for two days. With peanut meal, put directly in plastic bag and punch holes. Some like to use a dog food can with holes punched in it. Even a bar of Lifebouy soap can be effective. When I use chicken livers, I punch holes in the unopened plastic container. Two different types of bait that attract for a variety of fish is soybean cakes available from feed stores and old cheese obtained from commercial suppliers (listed under resources). It takes several pounds of cheese because it melts fast.

In the South, if one uses raw fish for bait in large rivers and lakes, there can be problems with logger-head turtles and alligators. Traps can be destroyed. I talked to one fisherman who saw a 100 pound turtle bring his six foot trap to the surface and shake it like a dog does with a toy. Be careful when dumping fish, water moccasins have been found in traps.

100 pounds of catfish were caught in three days with this trap.

TRAP LOCATIONS

To set most traps, commercial fishermen find a river with a medium to slow current and places traps near a drop-off. Place the mouth of the trap downstream. This is so a fish following the smell of the bait will be led into the mouth of the trap. Fish bottom habitat "structure" as in bass fishing. In lakes, set traps on old creek banks or river channel ledges just below top edge. A good choice is where a creek joins a river (try next to brush piles). If you can find a bottleneck in a river, place your trap in the tightest spot. Generally, I use a baited trap in lakes. For shallow streams, I drive the fish into a winged, unbaited trap. When setting a trap in a lake, place it parallel to the bank. The fish swim in a circle following the bank. Place on the windward side so wind ripples will circulate the bait. Wings will aid in directing the fish into the trap mouth.

There are several ways to keep a trap hidden. When fishing from a shore position, tie a light-weight string such as kite string to the main retrieval rope. Use mud to darken the string. Toss the trap out with the main rope and once it is underwater and out of sight, run the thin string to a tree root under water. The thin string will be difficult for anyone to find. Use the string to retrieve the rope and the rope to retrieve the trap. This works so well I once couldn't find my trap rope and had to drag the shoreline to expose the rope.

Commercial wire trap users tie an anchor rope to the closed end of the trap. While heading downstream they will drop an anchor (old tire rim), letting it sink while feeding out a 50 foot connecting rope. When the line becomes tight, they gently release the trap. For a collapsible hoop net, anchor ropes are used on both ends. When retrieving either type, use a drag line hook to find the trap rope and then the trap is retrieved. Very few outsiders ever find these traps. Before setting your trap, be sure to drag the area for obstructions or it may become tangled and lost.

A simple trap made with chicken wire and wire hoops.

TRAP WINGS

Trap wings are made of wire or netting and direct fish into a trap. They are "V" shaped with the trap placed at the narrow end of the "V". In shallow water, vertical stakes can be driven into the dirt. When bait is not used, fish can be herded into a trap with wings.

A trap may be used in conjunction with a driver. The driver goes upstream, then wades down, beating the water with sticks and throwing rocks in the water. The fish, while escaping the driver, will concentrate at the trap. A variation of this trap can be used where fish approach the banks and shallows in the morning and evening. A wing is placed perpendicular along the shoreline. As the fish follow the shoreline they are turned toward deep water and into the trap.

TRAP TYPES

Hoop Traps

Hoop traps are round with funnel entrances at one or both ends. A good material is 1/2" nylon netting or chicken wire. Rings or hoops of a large gauge wire or fiberglass are made into 24" diameter circles. These hoops are wired around the cylinder at 1-2 foot intervals to maintain the circular shape. The funnel entrance narrows to approximately the size of the fish you are seeking. I use a 5 inch diameter opening shaped into a vertical oval. The opening should point down, level with the floor of the trap. By making the trap oval in shape, the trap will be less likely to roll upside down. In commercial models, there are two funnel entrances in one end to insure capture. Most commercial models use netting rather than wire allowing them to collapse for storage and transportation.

Commercially made collapsible hoop traps.

Welded Wire Trap

A welded wire trap normally uses a 1 inch mesh wire. The trap is fabricated into a Quonset hut shape with the flat side down. "Pig ear" tag clips" found at feed stores are used to bind/clip the edges together. The second funnel has a one-way horizontally hinged trap door making it very effective. The fish will push the door open to gain access to the bait but then can not exit.

Wood Stake or Willow Fish Funnel Trap

There are various wood stake funnel or maize traps that can be used as survival fish traps. Unfortunately they are very labor intensive to construct and they are not portable. Basically the trap allows the fish to enter but not allowing them to escape. A V-shaped barrier lead or wing, 10 feet long (unless the stream is too small) directs fish into the trap. The wings can be placed on both ends of the trap to increase the effectiveness but the openings need to be offset so the fish will not pass straight through the trap and out the other end. This type of trap can be made from a variety of materials. One good material is willow shoots. Shoots approximately 1 inch in diameter are driven into the stream bottom wide enough apart to allow water to flow though but close enough to stop the size fish you are trapping. The tops must stick out of the water. Stretching a net around shoots or weaving in of horizontal smaller shoots will reduce the quantity of vertical shoots needed and conserve considerable energy. In shallow water, place a barrier pile of brush place into the stream and weight down with stones. For larger waterways, use willow traps in the shallow areas just below a set of riffles or shallow pools. Choose a location where the stream is shallow enough and wide enough so the current is dispersed and manageable.

Willow maize trap.

Willow Hoop Open Throat Traps

A fish funnel can be made from young saplings or willow shoots and it is rather simple to fabricate.

Bamboo can be used if no willows are available. Bamboo bends better if you warm it. You'll need about 50 or so

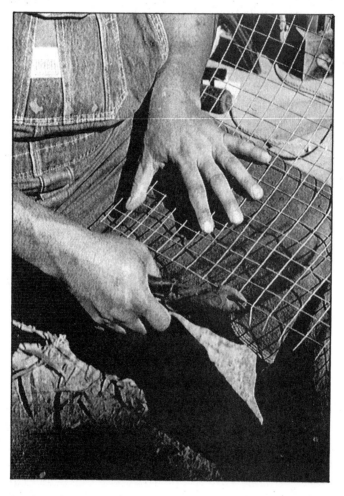

Traps are constructed from welded wire and held together with wire clips.

willow saplings, approximately 4-4 1/2 feet in length, and about as big around as your index finger. Collect the straighter young shoots growing in the center of the willow stand. After the shoots are cut to the same length, use string, cloth or the bark stripped off another stem to bind the saplings together with the smaller ends facing the same direction. Roll the woven saplings into a circle and lace the two joining edges together. The thinner ends are squeezed together and bound. Now the trap will be round, closed on one end and open on the other end. Similiar to the following "slat traps" but the trap will be round with no fingers to keep the fish inside once caught. The binding and lacing will continue to be pliable as long as it is kept in the water. Using wings or a large funnel to drive the fish into the trap makes the trap more effective. Jerk trap out when fish swim in. The same trap can be used with several sharpened "fingers or spears" of willow laced into place creating a funnel to keep the fish from swimming out. Obviously, the fingers or funnel are more effective than a plain open throat trap. You will only need about half the number of "finger or spears" as the total number of willows in the circumference of the trap. They point inward allowing the fish to slip in but not out.

Slat Traps

Slat traps are made from wood slats. Many feel they are one of the most productive traps because they are made from natural materials and offer a darkened interior. They are similar to a square-ended vegetable crate with a funnel entrance at one end. The side slats are spaced 1/4 inch apart. Once the wood becomes water logged, it will sink without a weight. Commercial versions have a throat made from plastic. The throat may be purchased separately from the suppliers listed later.

A slat trap using a wood and plastic throat.

Rock Maize Traps

Rock traps can be used rather the wood stakes or shoots to funnel fish into pen-barriers. When built across shallow creeks and small rivers, they work well. They are labor intensive but they are effective and do not require special tools or materials.

Many commercial fishermen use spoiled cheese for bait.

CONCLUSION

Trapping fish provides an efficient method to put fish on the table. Your chance of success will be greater by experimenting with different traps and bait. When used properly, trapping fish can be very productive. The most effective trapping techniques are those made and practiced in advance when both materials and tools are available.

Survival Tip: Utilize all fish caught. Even very small pan fish can be eaten in a survival situation. They are scaled, gutted, head removed and run through a meat grinder, bones and all to make fish patties. Or they can be dried in the sun, pounded with a rock, and used in fish chowder.

RESOURCES

Commercial Trap and Bait Suppliers:

The Fish Net Company - PO Box 462, Jonesville, LA 71343

Champlin Net Company - PO Box 788, Jonesville, LA 71343

Memphis Net & Twine Company - PO Box 8331, Memphis, TN 38108

CHAPTER IX

NATURE'S FREE FOODS

EATING WILD FOODS

Many wild edibles make good trailside snacks and add variety to home and camp cooking. We are going to discuss three wild edibles that grow throughout the United States, are readily found, and are easy to identify. All three can be eaten fresh or cooked while on the trail. Almost any trail recipe in which you would use garden greens can use these wild edibles.

This information is extracted for my book *God's Free Harvest–Successful Harvesting of Nature's Free Foods*. I hope this "taste" of nature'free foods will prompt you to explore this outstanding food source. Wild foods are a renewable resource that are nutritious, pesticide free, and available just outside your back door.

Some are against tasting wild edibles for wild edibles are not something they see in the produce section of the grocery store and they fear being poisoned by a misidentified plant. Actually most edible wild plants are easy to identify by a knowledgeable forager.

CAUTION: The identification and use of wild edibles as a food source should be done with care and attention to details as some plants are toxic. Always use several field guides in the identification process to insure proper identification. Before eating any wild plants, you should have been field trained by an expert. If this is not possible, then take the plant to an expert or botanist for positive identification. Even after the above precautions, the forager should initially taste only small amounts of the plant in question. You should then wait several hours before tasting more.

In general, young plants are less bitter than mature ones. Most mature wild plants will require a quick precooking in boiling water, then draining and final boiling to remove most of the bitterness or strong taste. If the wild edible has become woody or fibrous, it can be pureed and pressed through a sieve to exclude its fiber and then the liquid can be mixed into a soup or a cream sauce. Many like to mix their greens when making a fresh salad. By mixing greens, one can tone down a strong tasting green and/or add more taste to a bland green.

In a survival situation, tougher leaves and stems can be chewed and the juice swallowed then spit out the pulp.

Enough of general information! Let's learn about our three wild edibles: Brambles, wild grapes, and greenbrier.

CATTAIL

IDENTIFICATION

Cattails have long firm stalks, each topped with a dense sausage-shaped seed cluster that appears after the flowers fall off. The seed stalk grows to eight feet in height. Cattails are found widely in wet ground, ponds, and swamps where they create large colonies.

Survival Tips: Cattails are a year-round survival food abundant in ditches, through low water areas, and around ponds.

TUBERS/ROOTS

Gather cattail roots any time of the year. They are best when gathered from late fall through early spring when the starch is concentrated in the roots. After spring, the roots slowly shrink, harden, and become ropelike. Studies show that the roots are very good at absorbing chemical pollutants so do not collect in such water.

When baking, many prefer to mix cattail starch/flour with an equal mixture of wheat flour. To process the starch out of the roots, crush them in cold water. Next, pour the liquid through a sieve to separate out the fiber. Allow the liquid to sit until the white starch settles to the bottom, and then pour off the clear surface liquid. Add new water, stir, and repeat the process several times until all the fiber and particles are removed. After the final pouring off of the liquid, the remaining starch can be used wet as thickener or stored after being dried in the sun. Or roots can be dried in the sun for a week until they crack. Grind into flour and sift out the fibers.

I made my first cattail starch while on duty after Hurricane Hugo in Sumter, South Carolina. During the day I collected roots and at night in the privacy of my motel room, I processed the roots into starch. With a minimum of effort, I had a motel glass full of liquid starch. The most difficult part of the process was making sure no one saw me unload the roots into the motel room! Also, I sometimes wonder what the maid thought the next morning about the waste basket full of leaves and roots. K.L.

Cattail - Typha spp.

Outdoor Tip: Cattail roots are a rich source of carbohydrates. To prepare a gruel, scrape, clean, cut into pieces and remove large fibers from the cattail roots, then boil them to the desired thickness. To make a sweetener, crush roots in water, then strain and boil them down into a syrupy liquid of marginal sweetness. To make a flour, dry the roots thoroughly, skin them, remove fibers, and pound.

CORMS (Sprouts)

The corms are gathered during late summer to winter. The white horn-shaped corms grow along the root's length at the base of the cattail. Cook new corms like a potato. At the base of each sprout is a lump of tender starch material that is also cooked. The white baby shoots, emerging from the horizontal rhizome, are tender and tasty in salads.

SHOOTS

Gather shoots during the spring. The green shoots grow out of last year's dead stubble and are easy to collect when about two feet tall. Reach down to the base of the leaves and pull while twisting the shoot. The top of the plant above the roots will break off leaving the green leaves and the white inner shoot. Peel off the outer layers until the tender white core is reached. Boil or steam for ten minutes if you like them crispy or boil longer to make them softer. They have a flavor similar to cucumbers. Also, shoots may be chopped into 1/2 inch lengths and added to a stew. To freeze, blanch for two minutes, drain, pat dry, and place in plastic bags.

I was once swapping wild foods information with a family that was knowledgeable in food storage techniques. They were teaching me food storage while I was showing them how to use cattail shoots. I had always boiled my shoots, but that night I decided to stir-fry them. I was sure I had enough for a meal, but right before our eyes, the meal dissolved into nothing. It would seem the shoots are mostly water, and the heat had evaporated the water. Another case of the importance of practicing what you "think" will work before going on stage with it! Now, I only boil my shoots. K.L.

Survival Tip: Water can be obtained from young cattail shoots by chewing them to remove the liquid and spitting out the pulp. They make an especially good water source when they are growing in moist ground with no surface water to contaminate them.

Caution: Learn to distinguish young cattail shoots from the poisonous look-alike iris shoots. To do so is very simple. Iris shoots have sharp-pointed leaves unlike the rounded tips of cattail leaves. Later, iris produces colorful flowers in contrast to the sausage-shaped seed cluster of a cattail. Iris roots are unpleasant tasting in contrast to the bland taste of cattail roots.

Survival Tip: The root fibers and cattail leaves can be twisted into cordage. Cattail leaves make an excellent weaving material for mats and baskets. Equally important, dried cattail flower stalks make good dry bedding which can be found most of the year.

FLOWER SPIKES

Gather flower spikes during late spring. The immature flower spikes or flower buds should be gathered while still young and green. Husk papery bud sheath and boil in salty water for about ten minutes or until tender (some prefer to cook them still in the husk). Serve with butter and eat the flower head from its tough inner core like corn on the cob; otherwise, scrape or cut it off the core. The flavor is similar to corn.

SEEDS

Cattail seeds are collected during the summer. The lower female section of the cattail pod produces the seeds. Mature seeds can be mashed into a flour that is rich in protein. If the silky part of the seed mass is bothersome, it can be ignited and carefully burned off while helpfully parching the seeds. The tiny seeds may be softened by boiling.

Outdoor Tip: The down, or fluff, from mature cattail seed heads makes good fire tinder. It can be used for stuffing a pillow or as an insulator for warmth when layered between two pieces of material or stuffed into clothing or socks. The fluff was actually used in the Mae West life jackets for flotation! Even to provide light, cattail seed heads can be dipped into fat and ignited as a torch.

POLLEN

Cattail pollen is produced during early spring. The seed head is divided into two parts with the male portion located above the female. To process, rub, strip, or shake the yellow male pollen into a bag. This substance is sweet and makes a good protein booster but it has a musty flavor and renders pastry products yellow. Sift the fine powder and use with wheat flour in breads and pancakes or alone as a thickener in soups. The pollen can be eaten raw or boiled in water for one-half hour until it thickens into a hot cereal. To store, keep the pollen in the freezer for several months, or it can be dried for future use.

Survival Tip: Protein-rich cattail pollen can be eaten raw–this is an important advantage if there are no cooking means available.

GRAPES

IDENTIFICATION

Grapes have broad heart-shaped, velvety, simple leaves with saw-toothed edges. The leaves are often lobed (having extensions), and the branches with tendrils can be high climbing or trailing in effect. The stems have a scaling nature. The small green flowers produce a cluster of round grapes which at maturity range from 1/4 inch to 3/4 inch in diameter and have 1-4 round, pear-shaped seeds. Grapes are found throughout the United States in moist, fertile soil along the edge of woods, where they can climb.

Warning: Grape roots are poisonous as are the berries of Canada moonseed or bittersweet nightshade with which grapes may be confused.

Canada moonseed has no tendrils, and there is only one crescent-shaped seed in its bitter black berry. The leaf is not attached directly to the leaf stem; instead, the stem intersects under the leaf. The leaf is smooth edged.

Bittersweet nightshade has a trailing vine with a woody stem. The leaf has two lobes (leaf extensions)

Wild Grapes - Vitis spp.

where it intersects the stem. The berries are red, bitter, and oval rather than round.

LEAVES

The leaves may be used early spring through summer. Young, tender, full-sized leaves can be cooked as a vegetable or green and the very young leaves can be eaten raw. The leaves boiled for a short time to soften them and can be used to wrap meat or rice for baking–a procedure that gives a subtle acidic or lemony flavor to the encased foods.

Medicinal Tip: A tea made from the leaves can be used for diarrhea and stomachaches. Also, native Americans made a poultice from the leaves for headaches and fevers.

TENDRILS

The tendrils maybe gathered during early summer and can nibbled raw or cooked as a vegetable.

SHOOTS

The young shoots maybe used spring through summer. They can be cooked like asparagus or with other foods to add texture.

Survival Tip: Military manuals say that a drinkable liquid can be obtained from grape vines during the summer. If the vines are cut off near to the ground and higher up the vine, sap will drip from the severed vine. I have found that the vine must be in very moist ground or near water to produce a liquid.

FRUITS

The fruit is gathered late summer through fall. It is used to make juice or jelly or for eating raw. The rind of muscadines and scuppernongs can be used to make pies. Normally wild grapes are not as sweet as domestic grapes. In addition, the young, unripe fruits can be used as a source of pectin to jell various foods.

Medicinal Tip: Grape fruits are slightly diuretic and can be used as a mild laxative. Some sources indicate that grape juice taken in large quantities will control diarrhea.

GREENBRIER

IDENTIFICATION

Greenbrier has thorny semi-woody, climbing vines with tendrils. The variformed leaves tend to be round or oval in shape. They are leathery with the veins running parallel. In temperate areas, one will find the plant still green in the winter. The fruit is small, black with a bluish tint, and grouped in little clusters. Two of the most well-known varieties are Common greenbrier and Bullbrier greenbrier. Common greenbrier has broad heart-shaped leaves and very thorny stems. Bullbrier greenbrier has triangular heart-shaped leaves, larger shoots and roots, and stems that are less thorny. Greenbrier is found throughout the United States in open woods and bottom land.

I found greenbrier entirely by accident. While at work I was complaining about a plant invading my woods at

Greenbrier - Graminiae spp.

home and how its thorns would tear skin and clothes. A good friend said I must have a crop of greenbrier. The name had a familiar sound, so that afternoon, I found that greenbrier was one of the plants on my list to research. I now cherish cooking the tasty young tips every spring. If you have ever had your clothing snagged by the thorns of a green, semi-wood vine while in the woods, you have met a greenbrier! K.L.

Survival Tip: Good cordage can be made by braiding together several strands of greenbrier, though this cordage becomes brittle when dried. Its larger thorns make effective spur attachments for hooks and fish spears. Greenbrier shoots make a nutritious uncooked trail food.

LEAVES

The young leaves can be harvested from spring through summer and eaten raw or cooked as a vegetable.

SHOOTS AND TENDRILS

The young shoots are, also, collected from spring through summer and are eaten raw or cooked to eat like asparagus, with butter.

CONCLUSION

As in any new venture, one may feel unsure where to begin. By experimenting with three simple wild foods, one can enjoy learning a new and rewarding hobby and survival skill.

A new wild food "find" is cooked back at camp.

CHAPTER X

HOW TO USE INSECTS AS FOOD

Insects are being eaten in most of the world. Archaeological evidence tells us that entomophagy has been practiced since mankind first made an appearance on this planet. It would appear that all levels of society consumed various insects and today they remain an important food source in many parts of the world

Of course, for the average person, a good steak and a salad would be your first choice, but during uncertain times it is always good to have alternatives such as insects. Insects are low in carbohydrates and high in protein, fat, and calories, which are needed in a survival situation. For example, crickets and grasshoppers have approximately 24 percent protein. Grasshoppers have 200 calories per 100 grams (approximately 900 calories per pound and some studies show up to 1,200 calories per pound) with 7-9 percent fat, compared to steak at 250 calories per 100 grams. Also, crickets have amino acids required in the human diet. Beef provides 200-300 calories per 100 grams with 18 percent protein and 18 percent fat.

Unfortunately, they do not weigh much and it will take a rather large quantity to feed you. However, they can be a food of opportunity - so if you find them, use them. Also, they do not need to be the main course of a meal. You may only find a few of this and that type of insect, so mix and match and use them all.

In a food shortage situation, raising insects such as crickets (normally raised for fish bait) takes minimal space; they are quiet and are not very demanding in food requirements. Go to a live fish bait store and learn from them.

Unfortunately, most of what we eat has a cultural basis. For example, have you eaten brains and eggs? In addition, when anything is prepared in a readily acceptable form, it can be consumed without any problem. For example, if an insect was dried, ground and added to flour, then used in soup as thickener or to fortify bread, cakes and other flour based food, no one would be the wiser.

We now consume red dye 56, MSG and a variety of other additives without even a thought of their source or what they can do to our bodies. Insects are what they eat, which is more appetizing than what catfish and shellfish eat, or even pigs.

INSECT NUTRITION

Insect nutrition varies from source to source, but the bottom line is that they are nutritious. At the United States Air Force Air War College in Montgomery, Alabama, I found the following information in Survival Nutrition Information Bulletin #8 - Insects as a Food Source of Nutrients.

Insects	Nutritive Value
Termites	Protein (36%), 350 calories per 100 grams, 28 % fat.
Caterpillars (smooth skin)	Fat (13.7%), Carbohydrates (6.1%) - Any type eating nontoxic plants
Earthworms	Protein (70% dry weight)

Silkworm and Pupae	Vitamin A, Fat (14.2%), Minerals (15%)
Larvae	Protein (23.1%), Water (60.7%)
Locusts	Protein, Fat, Ca, S, Fe
Grasshoppers	Vitamins B1, B2
Grubs	Protein, Fat
Water Bugs	Protein (38.1%), Fat (6.1%)

EDIBLE INSECTS

Now that you have some background information, let us explore the edible insect world. The following is provided for informational purposes only. Experiment at your own risk. I have tried many, but not all, of the following.

Amphibians

Although not insects, salamanders, frogs and tadpoles are edible. Avoid frogs that are brightly colored or that have a distinct "X" on their backs. Do not eat toads because some emit poisons through their skins.

Ants

Ants and ant larvae are edible and tasty. The formic acid mostly disappears when they are boiled. Black ants can be eaten raw. Fire ants are not considered to be edible.

Beetles

Both the adults and larvae of cicadas, Japanese beetles, June bugs and floor beetles are edible.

Caterpillars

Caterpillars are edible but the smooth ones are best to use. Survival manuals recommend not eating the brightly colored caterpillars. However, the brightly colored tomato worm is edible.

Cockroaches

It may be hard to believe, but cockroaches are edible. Some military manuals indicate nutrition is low. Obviously, they are a prime candidate for gut purging due to their poor food source. To purge, keep them contained in a fisherman's cricket tube or a cricket raising box for several days. Use water and a good food source to purge their systems. Try wet lettuce or piece of apple. Remember, cockroaches are fast and they can fly. When you're ready to eat them, put them in the freezer to kill, then remove heads, legs and wings and cook them. You will find that some have an odor. Also, this is one insect that must be cooked due to parasitic worms they carry. To make the idea of eating a cockroach a bit more palatable, the specimens should be baked dry and ground into flour for mixing with a soup.

Crickets and Grasshoppers

Crickets and grasshoppers can add protein, calories, fat and variety to a meager diet. Crickets are my favorite, especially when stir fried in butter and garlic salt. Crickets can include mole crickets and Mormon crickets. Grasshoppers are the most common insects eaten worldwide. All are edible at all stages of their life cycle.

Earthworms

Earthworms have a nice concentration of protein in a little package. They are entirely edible and abundant to collect. They are edible both raw and cooked. It is advisable to purge their system to remove soil. To purge, maintain them in a non-soil environment, such as a moist shredded newspaper, for 24 hours.

Fly Larvae

The faint of heart need not apply and should skip this section because fly larvae are maggots. There has been research into using fly larvae from the soldier fly to grow edible larvae for livestock. University of Georgia entomologist Craig Sheppard estimates that the waste from a standard 100,000-bird chicken house seeded with soldier fly eggs will produce 66 tons of animal feed larvae in five months. They can be cooked, dried and mixed in with conventional animal feeds. They have 42 percent protein. Maybe soon it will reach the grocery store shelves?

I have a friend who was in Korea and was involved in the orderly evacuation (retreat, as some would recall) as the Americans withdrew south. His was to insure that the convoy made the correct turn at major intersections. As the last of the convoy was making a turn, he asked the driver if he was the last truck. The driver thought there was one or two more stragglers. Finally, down the road, a lowboy with a tank on it rounded the turn. Unfortunately, the tank had a large red star on its side. He watched in dismay as the turret turned his way and realized it was time to run into the woods. A few seconds later, his only transportation south exploded. He later found a small village where he stayed for several months until the area was retaken by the Americans. After a diet of mostly rice, he heard the only oxen in the village had died. The thought of a steak dinner made him ecstatic. When he saw that they scraped maggots off the meat and into the rice, he decided he didn't want rice any more. To this day, my friend cannot eat rice - even one piece of rice on a steak will make him lose his appetite. Also, he says you can tell the maggots from the rice because the maggots look like a piece of rice with a black head.

Fly larvae are commercially available for biological research and as food for some pets. A local pet store may be a source of information. In nature, they are easy to capture and often found in clusters in such places as road kill. They are high in calories and protein.

One way to remove the larvae from decomposed meat is to place the meat in a box with openings in the bottom corners and containers under the openings. The larvae will crawl to the corners where they will fall into the containers. Bright lights seem to aid in driving the larvae off into the containers. When you've collected the larvae, wash in cool water and cook. Another method is to place larvae in an old sock and rinse in cool water a couple of times. Then remove larvae and boil for five minutes and add a bullion cube. When the cube is dissolved, you are ready for your stew.

Honey Bees

Honeybees are accepted around the world as a favored food. They are edible at all stages of growth (larval, pupae and adult). Boiling tends to break down their poison, which is basically protein, and at boiling temperatures, the stinger softens. Pounding them before boiling is effective.

Mealworms

Mealworms are easy to prepare and are tasty additions to any recipe. They, like crickets, have an oily, nutty flavor. One cup of mealworms weighs up to six ounces. Store and freeze the larvae in plastic bags for future use. Prepare as with other insects.

For a starter stock, they are readily available from pet dealers along with directions for raising them. The mealworms you purchase will be packaged with bran or newspaper. They are easy to raise if you have a source of bran meal. Begin with shoeboxes or plastic containers. Fill with four inches of bran meal or cream of wheat and add 25 or more mealworms. For the moisture and additional food required, place an apple or potato slice on top of the bran. Replace moisture source every seven to ten days. A thin layer of shredded paper is placed on the meal for the adult beetles to crawl on. No cover is needed because the beetles will not crawl out of the container. Add additional meal as needed. Excess gray granular waste material can be sifted out with a kitchen strainer. Once the pupa emerges into a beetle, it will lay 400-500 eggs that hatch into larvae in two weeks. The larvae grow to one inch long before they pupate. Then they become an adult beetle in two or three weeks.

In a survival situation mealworms will eat any crushed grain or weed seeds. Remember, a potato or other moist root or fruit best provides moisture.

Mayflies

Mayflies are edible and are good. Prepare as with other insects.

Moths

Moths that you find flying around your lights are edible and taste pretty good - a little bit like almonds. Prepare as with other insects. Moth larvae provide about 265 calories per 100 grams. They are about 63 percent protein and 15 percent fat. Unfortunately, it takes a lot of moths to make a pound.

Rolli-Pollies

These little insects are found under boards and rocks in moist places. They are crustaceans and related to lobsters. Boil in water and eat as a protein source. They have a crunchy texture.

Silverfish

Silverfish are edible. Prepare as with other insects.

Snails and Slugs

Snails and slugs are not insects, but they are a good food resource. Both aquatic and terrestrial snails are edible and an excellent source of food. According to an entomologist friend, slugs should be edible. He suggested they be boiled in vinegar to remove mucous, then stir-fried in butter and garlic salt.

Termites

Termites are the second most widely eaten insect in the world, next to grasshoppers. Tropical varieties are very large, while local varieties are normally too small. Termites in the Southeast are much smaller than in the Western United States. But if you find a collection under a log, as I have occasionally found, throw them in whatever is for dinner.

Water Bugs

Water bugs are edible

Wasps

Wasps are edible if thoroughly boiled to break down their poison, which is basically protein. Also, at boiling temperatures, the stinger softens. Pounding them before boiling is effective. Wasp larvae are delicious. Prepare as with other insects

PREPARATION BASICS

When preparing crickets, first remove any dead insects. Those that are alive will have to be slowed down by placing in a refrigerator for several hours. Remove and place in a kitchen colander and toss them while blowing or using a hair drier to separate the debris from the crickets. The small debris will pass through the colander and the other will blow away. Pour out the crickets on a paper towel or wax paper. If you have not removed the dead ones before putting in the refrigerator, then remove them now. Rinse in cool water, drain, pat dry with a paper towel and use immediately or freeze in a plastic bag for later use.

To use, you may or may not want to remove the legs and wings. Some recommend removing the heads because they have no food value but I prefer to not remove anything. If you prefer to remove parts, the procedure works best when the insect is frozen or already dry roasted.

Insects with a hard outer shell have parasites and a few are transferable to humans, so cook them before eating.

Grasshoppers, in particular, can carry several parasitic worms that can be passed to humans, as do beef. Most other insects can be eaten raw, but cooking normally improves their taste.

Do not eat insects such as spiders, mosquitoes and some ants, such as the fire ant or insects that have a pungent odor.

Insects are best if cooked or frozen while alive. Once insects die they can become unpalatable. Actually, insects can be kept alive for several days in a refrigerator. Freezing or refrigeration serves two purposes. The insects can be collected over a period of time until an adequate quantity is gathered, and the more lively insects will be slowed down for easier preparation.

Larvae are easier to eat than adult insects. This is because young insects are usually soft like caterpillars. The hard covering of most adult beetles and the wings and legs of most other adult insects are just too tough for most people's taste and therefore have to be removed. Not all adult insects are too crunchy to eat. Some insects, like crickets and grasshoppers, are soft enough to chew.

If you are concerned about what may be in an insect's gut, it can be purged. Allowing them to eat slices of apple, potato, pear or leafy vegetable for 24 hours can purge crickets and mealworms. Or to purge your insects before eating, separate them from their food for 24 hours. I do know that crickets and mealworms will turn cannibalistic, but some purging may be appropriate.

Soup

In general it is best to crush your insects and cook in a stew to disguise their appearance. If at any time you find you cannot eat an insect, do not despair. Boil the insects in a pot of water. The fat will rise to the top; scoop it up and drink it. Or, as is done in Japan with grasshoppers, boil in soy sauce to get a grasshopper that tastes sort of like a soy-sauce flavored potato chip.

Sauté

A favorite method to prepare insects is to sauté them. Melt butter, add garlic, sauté, for several minutes to blend flavors and then add insects. Sauté for an additional 10 minutes or until tender.

Dried

Insects placed on a paper towel can be baked on a cookie sheet at 150-200 degrees for one or more hours until dried. An alternative is to freeze the insects in a plastic bag overnight, then blanch them to remove any debris or contaminates. Next take off the head and legs and bake them for about two hours until dry. You will now have an insect that will fit into most recipes. In the outdoors, they can be killed and then placed on a hot rock to be solar dried.

Flour

After insects have been dried, they can be made into flour using a blender.

CHAPTER XI

SELF-SUFFICIENCY

PREVENTION OF FOOD SPOILAGE WHEN POWER GOES OUT

During a power outage, many do not realize that a freezer or refrigerator can be wrapped in blankets or insulation to extend its cold-holding capability. If a generator is used, operate several times a day to keep refrigerator cold.

Also, I read once about canning thawed food (still has ice crystals) to reduce losses. When I was working during Hurricane Hugo, over 20,000 families lost all their frozen food, including their annual shrimp harvest. No one thought about canning the thawing food.

The following food safety tips are provided by the Miami/Dade Cooperative Extension Service in preparation for Hurricane Andrew:

Set your refrigerator to the coolest setting, open only when absolutely necessary and close quickly. If you take these precautions, food can be preserved for up to two days without electricity.

A portable ice chest comes in handy as a substitute refrigerator to keep food and beverages cool and will reduce opening the refrigerator.

Even though it may seem wasteful, never eat any perishable foods such as meat, poultry, fish, milk and cheese that have been without refrigeration for more than several hours. It may seem fine, but could contain bacteria that can cause food poisoning.

Chopped meats like hamburger spoil quickly when not refrigerated; so does pork, fish and poultry. Throw them out if they've been uncooked for several hours; don't trust your sense of smell. Meats least likely to spoil are large, solid, unboned cuts like leg of lamb or rump roast.

Eggs will keep for several days in a cool place without refrigeration; hard cheese keeps well at room temperature. Cream cheese, open containers of cheese spread and cottage cheese spoil quickly.

Fresh milk spoils quickly without refrigeration.

Foods such as custard or creamed foods spoil very quickly and should be discarded.

Fruits and vegetables such as bananas, apples and citrus keep at room temperature for several days.

Also, if you fill the empty space in a freezer with water filled milk jugs, the freezing capacity is increased and the water is available when thawed.

Remember: Taste or smell cannot detect Botulism. When in doubt, throw it out. In addition, I would like to add that cooking thawed foods extends their life for the next several meals.

FOOD STORAGE

For temporary emergencies, your emergency supplies of canned goods and everyday foodstuffs should be adequate.

For major disasters and even an economic collapse, you may want a longer-term approach with additional supplies.

You have already read about bulk food storage but what do you do for those who arrive late to the party or for those with limited funds? Then I found a economical, simple and very basic diet to sustain life at a Spartan level.

A SPARTAN THREE GRAIN STORAGE SYSTEM

The following plan is very simple and one that anyone can afford. It also allows support groups to stock large quantities with minimum investment. It is based on storing just three dried grains (corn, wheat and soybeans) and some optional items.

Stock the following amounts per person per two months:

Dried Corn	50 lbs.
Wheat	50 lbs.
Soybeans	25 lbs. (Soybeans only come in 50 pound bags)
Salt	1 lb.
Vitamin C	30 grams (Rotate every two years)

Nice Additions:

Sugar/honey	5 lbs.
Multivitamin	60 day supply
Powered milk	40 lbs. Can be used for infants (If not in nitrogen packed cans, then rotate every six months)
Cooking oil	
Baking soda	
Baking powder	

The above will provide two months of basic food for one person, based on around 2500 calories a day. If these staples comprise your entire menu, you must eat all of them together to stay healthy. To avoid serious digestive problems, you will need to grind the corn and wheat into flour and cook them. A nutritiou bread can be made by grinding all three.

The beans will also need to be boiled before eating if not mixing into bread.

Vitamin C is added since it is lacking from the dried grains and beans. Fortunately, Vitamin C can be obtained by sprouting and wheat is especially good for this.

Also, sprouting beans or taking a teaspoon of apple cider vinegar removes the gas they produce. Other beans can be substituted but soybeans have more oil, absorb the flavor of what they are cooked with and they can be used to produce soy milk for babies (see soy milk recipe).

One pound of salt and sugar are more than needed but extra salt may be needed and sugar makes food palatable and adds extra needed calories to the diet. The average American consumes over 100 pounds of sugar a year. It stores well and it's a great barter item. Keep it dry and away from ants and rats.

Glass jugs have the advantage of not rusting but the disadvantage of being breakable. They should be kept it a dark place or covered with dark paper or plastic to exclude light.

For this program, a wheat mill or a method of grinding is needed but not mandatory. Also, if you have power, a blender can produce flour making coarse bread. Many health-food stores sell hand-crank grain mills or they can tell you where you can get one. Make sure you buy one that can grind whole corn. Metal bur types can also grind soybeans, which can clog up a stone mill.

R & R Mill Company (P.O. Box 187, Smithfield, UT 84335) sells an inexpensive Corona grain mill.

If you do not have a grain mill, you can crush your grain by filling a large can with whole grain one inch deep, holding the can on the ground between your feet and pounding the grain with 3 lenghts of 3/4 inch ordinary water pipe. Pipe held together with duct tape. Encircle each pipe with slip-preventing tape. The multiple pipe ends speeds up the milling process.

Unfortunately, whenever someone eats the same food repeatedly, appetite fatigue develops. In some cases, they would rather starve than eat the same food again.

Also, the psychological shock of an emergency will cause many people to reject unusual foods and go hungry. This is especially true of young and older people. It has been documented that during war, many children and aged persons have starved to death rather than adjust to unfamiliar foods.

We can learn from history. Under adverse conditions, we must try to make life as normal as possible. Variety is the key to your program, so plan to add additional foods as you can.

ANIMAL FEED GRADE GRAINS

Notice: The following is provided for informational purposes only. Most authorities recommend using only food grade grains and beans. You will have to make your own conclusion.

Bulk storage grains will last 5-15 years if stored properly. Unfortunately, food grade grains are expensive. For example, corn in a plastic bucket can cost $32.00 for 40 pounds plus shipping. On the other hand is the low cost of animal feed grade grains available from a feed store. In 1999, for example, a 50 pound bag of feed corn only costs $5.25 and you do not have the large freight bill associated with special order grains.

According to the Georgia Department of Agriculture Grain Grading Lab, both food grade and feed grade grains are tested the same. The primary difference in food and feed grades is the extent of cleaning. Both are stored, shipped and fumigated the same. For example, in corn, aslatoxin is dangerous and this is tested at 20 parts per billion for both food and feed grades.

The scientist at the lab stated than when grain is cleaned, removing the debris, dirt etc. (commercially or done by an individual), the aslatoxin is substantially reduced through the cleaning process. He also said that as grain comes to the feed mill by truck or rail car, it is tested by the mill's quality control personnel. If the grain is for feed, it is ground after testing. When for food use, they just "blow it out" and then grind it.

In most cases, feed grains move through the system much faster than food grains, they are usually fresher and have no need for any storage or fumigation.

The Purina Feeds scientist told me all their feed grade corn is tested for aslatoxin. He said wheat and soybeans are already safe.

Be aware, any corn that does not pass quality control is used for things like deer or wildlife feed. So don't use any corn used for deer feed.

Using the black light to test for bad molds is not effective because all molds will glow. But if it glows a great deal, you may have a problem. Also, grind the corn first and then test it to get the best analysis.

Any USDA testing lab will test sample grains for no charge, as long as an individual, and not a company, submits it. Call any local feed mill to get a contact.

Bulk seed wheat (untreated), feed corn and feed soybeans are obtained from a farmer's supply. Buy fifty-pound bags of each. Feed wheat can be used but it may have bits of corn in it from harvesting other fields where seed wheat is not pure. (In the south they only handle soft winter wheat for feed and planting. This type of wheat is low in gluten but will do in an emergency and makes reasonably good bread).

Also, for hard winter wheat, check with local health food stores, food co-ops, special order grocery stores, or with someone you know who grinds their own flour. Unfortunately, shipping can become a significant factor on small orders.

SPARTAN RECIPES FOR BULK STORAGE

When using the Spartan Three Grain Storage System, your variety of recipes is limited. Here are recipes using very basic ingredients lacking commercial yeast or sourdough starter.

WHEAT

Cereal

1 C. coarsely ground wheat and 2 C. water.

The coarsely ground grain is added to boiling water and cooked 20 minutes to make two servings. Wheat and corn can be mixed to make a complete protein.

Cereal

2 C. water, 1/2 tsp. salt and 1 cup whole-wheat berries.

Cook several hours on low heat until soft. Soaking for several hours speeds the process.

Wheat Crackers

1 C. flour, 1 C. water and 1/2 tsp. salt

Mix ingredients into a thin batter. Spread on an oiled cookie sheet. Several cookie sheets can be done together to reduce oven use. Bake at 350 for 10 minutes and break into bite sized chunks when done.

Bulgur

1 C. wheat, 1C. water and 1/2 tsp. salt

Bulgur is basically steamed wheat. Use a large pot with lid, a rack and a smaller pot to go inside of the larger pot. Add water to just below the level of the rack. Place the smaller pot on the rack in the larger pot. Place 1 cup of wheat, 1 cup of water and 1/2 teaspoon of salt in the smaller pot and cover with a lid. Steam the wheat until it absorbs the water.

Bulgur can be made from whole kernel or cracked wheat and can be used as rice, mashed potatoes or baked to make a pleasant and nutritious crunchy snack. For a chewy breakfast cereal, try heating several cups of bulgur in 1/2 cup water and serve with milk and sweeten to taste.

Wheat Meat - Gluten

8 C. flour and 4 C. water.

Wheat meat is the term we use for imitation meat made from gluten. When dough is washed in water, the starch and bran are washed away, leaving gluten, an insoluble elastic mass. Though wheat meat is high in protein, it is not a complete protein and it is lacking in the amino acid lysine. Serve wheat meat with lysine sources such as eggs, beans, milk products, nutritional yeast, soy products and nuts.

You can use two pounds of whole-wheat flour to make 1 1/4 pounds of wheat meat. To prepare, take 8 cups of wheat flour and 4 cups of water and combine in a ball. Then knead and thoroughly beat for 10-15 minutes. Aggressiveness improves the results. Cover the mass with cold water for one hour. Then take the dough in your hands and wash out the starch in hot running water. After the starch is removed, the dough will be firm. Continue rinsing until the sandy feeling grain has been washed out. Let drain 30 minutes more. A 200 degree oven can be used to dry if too wet.

To cook and flavor the gluten, roll and cut into strips or make patties, add meat juices or soy sauce and boil in the flavor. Or the strips can be fried in the seasoning.

Tortillas

2 C. flour, 3/4 tsp. salt, 2 T. oil and 2/3 C. warm water.

Sift flour and salt into mixing bowl. Mix in oil. Blend in lukewarm water. Knead well on a lightly floured board. Make 12 equal balls from the dough. Cover with a cloth and let set for 15 minutes. Roll each ball into a round thin tortilla about 8" in diameter. Place tortilla on a moderately hot unoiled skillet. Cook until golden brown in spots and then turn over without breaking air bubbles.

Unleavened bread

4 C. flour

This is a bread made without any yeast or baking soda and therefore it does not rise. It will be dense like a cracker. It can be made in a pan and is sometimes called "pan bread" or "flat bread". It is a thin bread 1/4 to 3/8" thick.

To prepare, mix 4 cups of flour into a dough, adding enough water so that the dough mixes easily with a spoon, but not so much that it puddles on top. If too wet, just add more flour.

Allow the dough set a few hours, or overnight, to soften the coarser particles of flour. Temperature and the time the dough sets aren't critical, but keep the dough cool if you don't want sourdough. Take one half of the dough and spread into a no-stick frying pan. Then cover the pan with a homemade insulative cover of foil and a hot-pad on top. Cook at a low temperature until the topside is completely dry and then turn over and cook a few minutes more.

You will find unleavened baking more convenient than using yeast because you can just mix up flour and water and use anytime over the next couple of days.

A disadvantage of unleavened bread is that minerals such as zinc and calcium are less available than if yeasted. So if you're eating mostly unleavened bread, mineral supplementation might be a good idea.

CORN

Vegetable

1 C. corn, 3 C. water and salt to taste.

Soak dehydrated corn overnight. Add salt and cook slowly until tender. Corn will have a chewy texture similar to hominy.

Corn Tortillas

1 C. wheat flour, 1 C. cornmeal, 3/4 tsp. salt, 2 T. oil and 2/3 C. warm water.

Sift flour and salt into mixing bowl. Add other ingredients. Knead well on a lightly floured board. Make 12 equal balls from the dough. Roll out into a thin 8-inch tortilla. Heat oil in a large skillet until very hot. Fry each for 35-40 seconds.

Cornmeal Mush

1 C. cornmeal, 2 C. water and 1 tsp. salt.

Bring 1 C. water to a boil. Mix together the other cup of water and cornmeal and 1 teaspoon of salt. Slowly pour mixture into hot water. Cook for 20-30 minutes while stirring occasionally. Sweeten to taste and add milk, if available.

SOYBEANS

Dehydrated soybeans may be prepared as you would ordinary beans, but they need to be cooked longer (much longer) and they absorb the flavor of what they are cooked with. As to food value, they far exceed other beans. To prepare, place beans in a bowl and cover with water. General procedures are to soak several cups of soy beans for 12 hours or so while changing soak water several times.

Add fresh water and cook slowly for several hours or until soft. If using a pressure cooker, add water, salt and seasonings, cover and cook at 15 pounds pressure for 30-45 minutes. Then, crush the beans into a paste for use in recipes.

Adding salt to soaking beans prevents both souring and sprouting and may help with the normal stomach gases.

Cooked soybeans hold their shape more and do not become mealy as do other beans. Although soybeans are rich in fat, meat drippings or bacon may be added for flavor. The secret of any soybean dish is the proper seasoning, since the beans themselves are rather flat in taste and need added flavor.

Soy sauce, onion, celery or tomatoes are excellent for flavoring soybeans. Soybeans may be substituted in any of the dishes for which navy or lima beans are used. Soybeans are at their pinnacle of food value when sprouted.

Soy Flour

Soy flour is an easy and economical way to improve the protein content of baked products. It is easy to work with, however, soy contains neither gluten nor starch, so it must be mixed with other flours. Just adding a small amount to baked goods improves their flavor, helps preserve freshness and adds a nutty flavor.

Soy flour can be made from raw ground soybeans, but must be processed (generally toasted) to remove the raw bean flavor and odor. This type soy flour is full of fats and not used in general baking.

Soy Milk

2 C. soybeans and 6 C. water.

Soy milk can be used in the place of regular milk. Soak several cups of soybeans for 12 hours or so while changing soak water several times. Crush the raw beans and add 6 cups of water. Cook in large pot for about an hour to make a foamy mixture. Put through a blender, if available, and then strain through cheesecloth. Use soon or refrigerate, if possible.

Soybean Meatloaf

1/3 soybeans and 2/3 meat or meat flavoring.

You may not have the meat to use this recipe, but this is my favorite use of soybeans. Cook soybeans and allow to set overnight. In your normal recipe add 1/3 soybeans and 2/3 meat. You will have a moist and delicious meatloaf, which is fortified with protein and the cost reduced. Experiment using up to 2/3 soybeans for even greater savings.

Bean Bread

4 C. cornmeal, 2 C. hot water, 2 C. cooked and crushed beans and 1/2 tsp. baking soda.

Mix the cornmeal and soybeans. Then add soda and hot water. Mix well and form into balls. Cook in boiling water for about 45 minutes or until done.

Soybean Nuts

Dried soybeans can be made into a salted, toasted nut. They can be used as topping for desserts, in baking, salads or use as a snack.

To toast nuts, place prepared soybeans in a large, shallow baking sheet and bake at 200 degrees for approximately 30 minutes. Remove when golden brown; sprinkle with salt.

BEANS

Beans don't require bacon, salt pork, or ham hocks for flavor. They help, but might not be available if the stores aren't open. Vegetarian beans are healthier, anyway.

Beans are a very bland food. That is why the cultures which use beans as a mainstay are big on seasonings, and all of us should follow their example. Bay leaves, cumin, chili powder, garlic, onions (garlic powder/onion powder, or dried flakes), Italian seasonings (e.g. oregano), as well as maple syrup, sugar and tomato sauce can be used to flavor beans.

If fuel is a concern when cooking beans, here are my suggestions. The best would be to cook on top of a wood stove, Dutch-oven/campfire or fireplace. Propane is an option, but any way you look at it, it's going to be at least a couple of hours of propane cooking. One way to be as efficient as possible is to cook a lot of the dried beans and can them. Then it will be a simple matter of grinding them. In a health food store, I've bought dehydrated refried beans. Dehydration may be something to try.

About half-way through the cooking process, I usually add some rice, whose protein compliments that of the beans to make a nutritionally complete protein for use in building human bodies umpteen ways.

Dried beans can be ground into flour and substituted for part of the wheat in making bread, rolls, and biscuits (around 1 cup bean flour for 1 cup wheat flour). This adds nutritional value and compliments the wheat protein, just like the beans and rice.

You can use cooked pinto beans to make a great sweet pinto bean pie. Just make your typical recipe for pecan pie, only instead of using pecans, use pintos. When served to others, they will be dubious about the first bite. Afterwards, they will ask for more.

Cooked beans in spaghetti sauce, with perhaps some dried or fresh shredded carrot and squash, is a great topping for any kind of pasta.

In fact, one can tend to think of pinto beans as a general all-around substitute for hamburger. They can even be substituted for a meat pie (Bean Shepherd's Pie has received rave reviews) or even substitute for sandwiches.

Thus far, we have hardly even touched on the wide variety of Mexican dishes that use beans, but the possibilities here include burritos, enchiladas and tostados. Even try beans for breakfast, over biscuits or on toast.

You can put onions, garlic, cumin, etc. in with the beans, but don't add salt or acidic things like tomatoes, or the beans will never soften. After they're cooked and soft (about 45 minutes) you can salt them and add dried ham soup base, and things like that, to season them.

MULTI-GRAIN BREADS

With a mill to grind the dried corn, soybeans and wheat into flour, you can make bread and many other dishes. A very tasty and nutritionally complete bread, containing all essential amino acids, can be made following this recipe. To improve the flavor of the soybeans, they can be toasted before grinding but they are still usable without toasting. Try both methods.

Three Grain Bread

2 cups dried corn, 2 cups wheat, 1 cup dried soybeans, 1/2 tsp. salt, 1/2 tsp. baking powder (if available), 1 cup water and 1 egg (if available)

Beat egg and add water. Mix baking powder, salt and 1 1/4 cup of multi-grain flour made from grinding corn, wheat and soybeans. Pour mixture into an oiled skillet and bake 20 minutes at 450 degrees. This recipe makes a heavy and flat bread.

Wheat and Beans Hamburger

1 C. wheat, 1 C. cooked soybeans and 1 egg (if available)

Boil whole-wheat berries 1 hour. Crush wheat and then crush beans and mix together with an egg. If a blender is available, blend the wheat and then add soybeans and blend together. Next mold the mixture into patties and season to taste. Grill or add to recipe using hamburger.

BOX COOKING TO SAVE FUEL

A major technique to minimize fuel use is thermal cooking, where one brings the pot/pressure cooker up to pressure quickly, then the pot is placed in an insulated container. The insulated container can be constructed simply from a box big enough to hold the pot. Newspaper can be used for insulation as a "sandwich" between the pot and the side of the box and a layer of heavy-duty aluminum foil to reflect the heat back to the pot.

Check out the soft-sided insulated picnic devices designed to keep food hot which can be used for this purpose. The food will continue cooking in the box.

Also, if you soak beans in water overnight, then cook them in a pressure cooker, it drastically reduces the amount of time and fuel required. Pressure-cooking requires much less water than the old open-pot method, and water will be a prime commodity.

The following is an article by Vicki Tate, author of "Cooking with Home Storage" (used with permission) I believe it will be beneficial for those just beginning a food storage program.

THE SEVEN MAJOR MISTAKES OF FOOD
STORAGE

A month or two ago I met a gal who was talking to me about her newly begun food storage. "You know," she began, "I've dreaded doing my storage for years, it seems so blah, but the way national events are going my husband and I decided we couldn't put it off anymore. And do you know it really hasn't been so hard. We just bought 20 bags of wheat, my husband found a place to get 60 pound cans of honey and now all we have to do is get a couple of cases of powdered milk. Could you tell me where to get the milk?" After I suggested several distributors, I asked, "Do you know how to cook with your wheat?"

"Oh," she laughed, "if we ever need it, I'll learn how. My kids only like white bread and I don't have a wheat grinder." She had just made every major mistake in storing food (other than not storing anything at all). But she's not alone. Through 14 years of helping people prepare, I've found most people's storage starts looking just like hers. So what's wrong with this storage plan? There are seven serious problems that may occur trying to live on these basics:

1. Variety

Most people don't have enough variety in their storage. Ninety-five percent of the people I've worked with have only stored the four basic items we mentioned earlier: wheat, milk, honey and salt. Statistics show most of us won't survive on such a diet for several reasons:

a. Many people are allergic to wheat and may not be aware of it until they are eating it meal after meal.

b. Wheat is too harsh for young children. They can tolerate it in small amounts, but not as their main staple.

c. We get tired of eating the same foods over and over and many times prefer not to eat than to sample that particular food again. This is called appetite fatigue. Young children and older people are particularly susceptible to it. Store less wheat than is generally suggested and put the difference into a variety of other grains, particular ones your family likes to eat. Also store a variety of beans. This will add variety of color, texture and flavor. Variety is the key to a successful storage program. It is essential that you store flavorings such as tomato, bouillon, cheese and onion.

Also, include a good supply of the spices you like to cook with. These flavorings and spices allow you to do many creative things with your grains and beans. Without them you are severely limited. One of the best suggestions I can give you is to buy a good food storage cookbook, go through it, and see what your family would really eat. Notice the ingredients as you do it. This will help you more than anything else to know what items to store.

2. Extended Staples

Few people get beyond storing the four basic items, but it's extremely important that you do so. Never put "all your eggs in one basket." Store dehydrated and/or freeze dried foods as well as home canned and "store bought" canned goods. Make sure you add cooking oil, shortening, baking powder, soda, yeast and powdered eggs. You can't cook even the most basic recipes without these items. Because of limited space, I won't list all the items that should be included in a well-balanced storage program.

3. Vitamins

Vitamins are important, especially if you have children, since children do not store body reserves of nutrients as adults do. A good quality multi-vitamin and vitamin C are the most vital. Others might be added as your budget permits.

4. Quick and Easy and "Psychological Foods"

Quick and easy foods help you through times when you are psychologically or physically unable to prepare your basic storage items. "No cook" foods, such as freeze-dried, are wonderful since they require little preparation. MRE's (Meal Ready to Eat), such as many preparedness outlets carry, canned goods, etc. are also very good. "Psychological Foods" are the 'goodies' - Jell-O, pudding, candy, etc. – you should add to your storage.

These may sound frivolous, but through the years I've talked with many people who have lived entirely on their storage for extended periods of time. Nearly all of them say these were the most helpful items in their storage to "normalize" their situations and make it more bearable. These are especially important if you have children.

5. Balance

Time and time again I've seen families buy all of their wheat, then buy all of another item and so on. Don't do that. It's important to keep well balanced as you build your storage. Buy several items, rather than a large quantity of one item. If something happens and you have to live on your present storage, you'll fare much better having one month supply of a variety of items than a year's supply of two or three items.

6. Containers

Always store your bulk foods in food storage containers. I have seen literally tons and tons of food thrown away because they were left in sacks, where they became highly susceptible to moisture, insects and rodents. If you are using plastic non food grade buckets, make sure they are lined with a food grade plastic liner available from companies that carry packaging supplies. Never use trash can liners as these are treated with pesticides. Don't stack them too high. In an earthquake they may topple, the lids pop open or they may crack. A better container is the #10 tin can which most preparedness companies use when they package their foods.

7. Use Your Storage

In all the years I've worked with preparedness, one of the biggest problems I've seen is people storing food and not knowing what to do with it. It's vital that you and your family become familiar with the things you are storing. You need to know how to prepare these foods. This is not something you want to have to learn under stress. Your family needs to be used to eating these foods.

A stressful period is not a good time to totally change your diet. Get a good food storage cookbook and learn to use these foods!

It's easy to solve the food storage problems once you know what they are. The lady I talked about at the beginning of the article left realizing that what she had stored was a good beginning but not enough, as she said, "It's better to find out the mistakes I've made now while there's still time to make corrections. This makes a lot more sense."

If you're one who needs to make some adjustments, that is OK. Look at these suggestions and add the things you need. It's easy to take a basic storage and add the essential items to make it livable, but it needs to be done. As I did the research for my cookbook, I wanted to include recipes that gave help to families no matter what they stored. As I put the material together, it was fascinating for me to learn that what the pioneers ate are the type of things we store. If you have stored only the basics, there's very, very little you can do with it. By adding even just a few things it greatly increases your options, and the prospect of your family surviving on it.

As I studied how the pioneers lived and ate, my whole feeling for food storage changed. I realized our "storage" is what most of the world has always lived on. If it's put together the right way, we will be returning to good basic foods with a few goodies thrown in.

A TRAPPER'S GRUB STAKE

I felt this information would be helpful in making a food storage list. These guidelines represent years of experience living away from modern conveniences and were written by Mr. Hawbaker in his book "Trapping North American Furbearers."

If fish and deer can be had, it will help the meat end considerably, although at least quite a few pounds of salt pork should be in every grub stake.

I will list a four month supply of food that will keep any trapper going for the given time, unless he actually wastes half of his grub in cooking or is a hog.

Flour	90 lbs.
Milk (condensed)	1 case
Butter	15 lbs.
Oat Meal	5-2 lb. boxes
Dried Eggs	3 lbs.
Tea	2 lbs.
Dried Fruits	30 lbs.
Onions	10 lbs.
Ketchup	2 large bottles
Beans	15 lbs.
Vanilla Flavoring	1 small bottle
Soda	2 lbs.
Salt	25 lbs (for cooking and jerking meat)
Cornstarch	2 boxes
Sugar	20 lbs.
Macaroni	2 lbs.
Lard	10 lbs.
Soap, laundry	5 bars
Soap, toilet	5 bars
Cheese	5 lbs.
Coffee	5 lbs.
Prepared Pancake Flour	6 lbs.
Cocoa	6 lbs.
Egg Noodles	4 lbs
Cornmeal	10 lbs.
Rice	6 lbs.
Jams	5 lbs.
Baking Powder	4 lbs.
Salt Pork	40 lbs.
Matches	Several large boxes
Yeast Cakes	4 packages
Black Pepper	2 lbs.

If one is tent camping, or intends to use only one cabin, this is a system that will work both in warm or freezing weather. Get a ten gallon can that has a good top lid and one that is waterproof. Make a place in the spring so that your can will be almost under water. Not any more than three inches should stick out. In order to sink the can, place rocks on the bottom of it. Then place your eggs, butter, milk, etc., into it and cover with burlap or a piece of blanket. Make sure your cover fits snugly and place a rock on the cover to keep animals or wind from knocking it off. The temperature of the spring water will keep the food cold in warm weather and, as a spring will not freeze, neither will the food.

DIATOMACEOUS EARTH - KILL CRITTERS IN BULK ITEMS

If you find that you prefer not to use the food preservation shown in the bulk food storage chapter, you may consider fossil flour. Fossil flour is a non-treated, non-milled, non-calcined fresh water form of diatomaceous earth. It consists of microscopic fresh water diatoms which were deposited millions of years ago and have since fossilized. Under microscopic examination, each particle looks like a tiny glass spear which pricks the outer skin or coating of insects, worms, maggots, etc. causing them to dehydrate and die. The product is a fine powder, white to gray in color. Diatomaceous earth is approved for use as an anti-caking agent in livestock and poultry feeds. It is used for long-term grain storage, insecticide on garden plants and as a wormer for goats. Test results (University of Illinois) in 1966 show that the use of the product does not harm animals or leave residues in milk or meat.

Diatomaceous earth is made up of the fossilized skeletons of tiny marine animals. It is not good to breathe, so you should be a little careful of that. Insects do not generally ingest it. When they crawl over it, it makes little scratches all over their bodies (exoskeletons) and causes them to dehydrate. It's that same action that makes it dangerous to your lungs. But it's fine to ingest in small quantities and it's also excellent in your animal's feed.

Diatomaceous earth is used at a ratio of 1/2 to 1 cup to 50 pounds of grain/product. Have someone sprinkle DE into the bucket as you fill it with grain to be stored. Seal tightly and roll or shake the bucket to cover all of the grain with the powder. Do not breath the dust.

There are two very different types of DE. One that is used as a filtering product (swimming pools) and NOT for animal or human use. It is hazardous to the lungs when breathed. The other is for agricultural purposes and as an additive for feed. The agricultural DE is not hazardous because of the different milling procedure.

As an insecticide, agricultural DE is a natural product and is safer than a garden poison. It is natural, non-toxic and very effective.

Fossil flour in 1999 is packed and priced as follows plus shipping:

2 Ibs.	$2.75
5 Ibs.	$4.40
10 Ibs.	$7.80

Nutritional Research Associates Inc.
P.O. Box 354, 407 E. Broad St., South Whitley, IN 48787
800-456-4931

Also available from:

> Gardens Alive - 812-537-8650 - gardener@gardens-alive.com

> Your local co-op or farmers' supply carry it both in bulk and under the "Concern" label for organic gardening.

STORING EGGS

During Hurricane Andrew I met two different seasoned sailors who regularly sailed for extended periods. One kept raw eggs in his 80-degree bilge water for up to four months. The other rubbed the raw eggshells with Vaseline and stored them on board for many months.

The following information is composed of email postings that I felt would be of interest.

Posting #1 - Cellar Eggs Keep 6 Months

My mom sells eggs to friends. They last at least 6 months. Mom tells her customers not to wash them. There is a coating on the eggs that will keep them fresh. Then keep them in the basement, which is a dark, cool, dry cellar. She said that was the way they did it when she was growing up.

Posting #2 - Egg Storage

The incredible, edible egg can be stored in the basement or fridge. The eggs need to be turned once a week. Just keep them in a carton and turn them over once a week. Mother Earth News did a test years ago and I believe they kept eggs for 6 months in a cellar just that way. To check and make sure the eggs are good put in water. Good eggs lie on the bottom, they do not float.

Posting #3 - Store Eggs with Waterglass

Waterglass (liquid sodium silicate) has several uses, one of them is for storing fresh eggs for extended periods of time. Here is a quote from Lehman's ad:

"Preserve eggs for months with waterglass. Mix one part waterglass with ten parts cooled, boiled water and pour into a large, stone crock. Wipe off fresh eggs with a flannel cloth and place in solution, with eggs covered with 2 inches of solution. Cover crock and store in a cool dry place."

Posting #4 - Store Eggs with Waterglass

We are the stewards of a flock of approximately 15 muscovy ducks. They lay between 100 and 120 eggs a year per hen. If we end up with 20 hens that we keep that means about 2,000 delicious eggs. Naturally I am concerned about storing eggs. So here is some of my egg research. I obtain sodium silicate solution from a local pharmacy. They can order it if they don't have it.

Here are the details of the method referred to as the waterglass method. Pack eggs that are between 24 hours and 4 days old. Older eggs don't keep as well. Eggs with no roosters or drakes around will keep longer than fertile eggs, but of course you then have to cope with unhappy roosters or drakes.

Boil the water and let it cool before you add the waterglass. Then pour the mixed solution into the crock. Remember not to fill the crock or container too full of the solution because you will be adding eggs, so no more than a third full. Add the eggs. Make certain that there is an extra 2 inches covering them. In hot weather it evaporates pretty fast, so watch it carefully. Earthenware, enamel, glass or plastic all work fine.

Cover the container as tightly as you can. Don't let it freeze but store it in a cool dark place. It starts out clear liquid but gradually turns cloudy into a milk colored sort of jelly. The book says it isn't harmful, but the container had all these "be careful" on the labels, so I asked the pharmacist and he said in a 1:9 ratio it has no harmful effects. It won't hurt you if you get it on your hands after it is mixed but I wore gloves to mix it.

Make up enough solution as you go to handle any new eggs you put in. So if you are putting in ten eggs, make sure there is enough to cover them, leaving 2 inches over the eggs. If it gets low due to evaporation, add some more solution that is mixed 1:9.

To use the eggs, you will have to wash them so the goop doesn't fall into the food or if you hard-boil them you should prick the small end so they don't pop. The sodium silicate works by sealing the eggs and should keep them for up to a year.

Here is a neat tidbit - don't wash the egg before preserving it because the egg is actually covered by a natural sealer. Without it, it is more susceptible to bacteria and evaporation. Any particularly dirty eggs wash and use right away. Don't use cracked eggs.

Eggs harvested between March and May keep better. I am is guessing that it's because of the milder temperature. To freeze eggs you should separate any that will need to be added to recipes separated or only needs egg whites. When we do this we put the extra yolks in the egg mixture we make. The freezer life is 8 months. Wash the eggs thoroughly, use very well cleaned utensils (not just something out of a drawer).

You will have to use them within 12 hours of thawing them, so keep your frozen packages small to avoid waste. I use baby food jars. Simply break the egg into a jar and label it as whole egg. If you do whites only for meringues or other recipes then be very careful that not even a speck of yolk gets in with them. Don't add anything to the whites.

1 1/2 Tbs. of thawed yolk equals 1 egg yolk
2 Tbs. of thawed egg white equals 1 egg white
3 Tbs. of whole egg equals 1 egg, more or less

WATER SAVING IDEAS AND SHOWERING TECHNIQUES

You quickly learn how wasteful you are with water once you lose it. Do you know it takes an entire 55-gallon drum of water to wash one load of laundry in all automatic washer?

I have two dish pans in my kitchen sink. The dirty dishes have been put into the cool rinse-water pan from the last washing to soak. I then put straight hot water into the dishwashing pan. As I wash the presoaked dishes, the water is accumulating in the washing pan. By the time the pre-soaked dishes are washed, the pan is about half full of water. I add the next batch and let them soak while the first batch air dries. The old rinse water is emptied into a five-gallon bucket. The second batch of dishes goes into the empty rinse pan. When I have a pan full, I begin to rinse the dishes, allowing the rinse water to accumulate in the pan. If the water gets too dirty or greasy, I just add it to the five-gallon bucket of wastewater, add soap to the rinse water, making it the new wash water and start off with fresh rinse water. At the end, the wastewater can be used on plants or for cleaning the porch.

Never run water when washing or bathing. Use enough to do the job, but don't let it run indiscriminately. It's amazing how much clean water goes down the drain.

I have also discovered a wonderful way to shower. I bought a new Hudson three-gallon spray tank like they use to spray chemicals on plants. That's why I bought a new one. Even a used one that was scrubbed thoroughly would have residual contamination. One teakettle of hot water to two gallons of cold water provides enough water for two showers. The tank stays outside the tub/shower. Just pump up the pressure according to the direction. Since the spray is a gentle mist, it uses a low volume of water. The flexible hose has the advantage of being able to spray exactly where you need it, making rinsing very efficient. The sprayer can also be used to mist seedlings.

We recently purchased one of those sun shower units, which is a vinyl solar-heated bag that holds one to five gallons of water.

HAND LAUNDRY AND CLOTHES WRINGERS

The following are some interesting email postings on hand washing of clothes.

Posting #1

As a young mother, I washed school clothes nightly by hand for my two school-aged children and their baby brother. Smaller items can just be wrung by hand. For heavier items, it helps if you have someone to assist you. Large pieces can be folded into thirds or fourths. Take two pieces of broom or mop handle about two feet long and insert them through the loops formed by the folds, then twist in opposite directions. In dry climates, it doesn't matter how well wrung your clothes are because they are going to dry in less than an hour, as a rule, especially on a sunny, windy day. I washed clothes by hand for most of my earlier married life.

We lived in the Western Utah desert in a railroad section settlement. My kitchen had a small wood stove. On washday, I'd get up, build a fire in the stove, fill the wash boiler with water and set it to heat on the stove. I started with whites and lightly soiled items first, then went to colored clothing and finally to work clothes and dungarees. They were rinsed in a sink full of cold tap water, wrung out, then were taken outside and spread on sagebrush to dry.

Areas with more humidity can expect a longer drying time. Winter in the central and northern tiers is usually quite dry, so if the weather is nice, you can hang clothes outdoors. (Don't forget to put CLOTHESPINS on your shopping list!) Freeze-drying clothing leaves them smelling exceptionally fresh and fragrant, too.

Posting #2

I live in a cold climate and the reality is that there will be a need at some point to hang clothing inside but here is what I learned in November with my dry-run (actually wet-run) using my wonder washer. I used the washer only for washing because I found the rinsing directions required 3 rinses and then there was still some soapy residue. I had two tubs of water set up and ready to go for rinsing.

Tools

Wonder Washer (pressure tank for clothes available from Emergency Essentials). Three laundry tubs (metal ones I got at an auction, cheap) or use two large plastic totes like a 20-30 gallon size and a sturdy rack that stands about 28 inches off the ground that put the tubs at a perfect height for rinsing. Two brand new toilet plungers, some salt and the cleaning stuff like bleach and soap. Kettle, siphon and barrel of water. 2x4 wringing bar attached between trees, with a home-made cotton cover to keep the clothes clean. Mine just ties around the 2x4. In the house in the basement I used a sturdy towel rack, but so far I've only done light weight clothes.

Procedure

I did this outside through November. I heated water over the fire while separating the clothes and hand scrubbing between my knuckles any bad stains. I dipped out of the pot the hot water recommended for the washer. I filled the one laundry tub with cold water and the other I used 1/2 cold and 1/2 boiling water and 4 tsp. of salt. I had the barrel of water with a siphon and long PVC end on it so I could just refill the water on the fire without lifting. The plastic tip of PVC protected the cheap plastic hose on the $1.99 siphon. You, of course, could use a garden hose if you have water pressure.

After spinning the clothes in the wonder washer so the soap penetrated the clothing, I removed the clothes, just lightly squeezing the garment to remove some of the soap, put it in the first tub (cold water) and continued adding each piece till the washer was empty.

While they soaked, I cleaned out the washer and prepared the next load. I left the clothes in the washer without the water and with the lid off until I was ready to hang up the first group. I used the plunger to concentrate on one garment at a time in the cold water rinse.

I took it out and looped it around the wringing bar and I twisted it with the water recovery tub under it. This kept me out of mud and I later used it to put out the fire and in the summer I could use the cleaner rinse water for the garden. After twisting it pretty dry, I put it in the second tub for the final rinse and let it soak while I washed the next load, then twisted each garment from the second rinse.

I then used the other plunger for that tub. I plunged each garment up and down a bit and then, one by one, took each item to the wringing bar and twisted them dry (only one item did I have to return to the second rinse because of excess soap). Before I hung them up, I emptied the washer and started that load soaking in the first tub. I checked the cleanliness of the rinse water to decide to fill the tubs [about every 3 loads, except heavily soiled jeans load] but added water as needed between dumping and wiping out the tubs. The salt keeps the clothes from sticking to the clothes line as the temperature hovers around freezing. Near the fire and with the activity level it was comfortable doing the laundry at 28 degrees and very little wind [on the cold day I did use heavy plastic gloves]. I have 5 clotheslines each 10 feet long and do jeans, socks, underwear, sheets, sweaters and shirts.

I did a total of 8 wonder wash loads (probably 4 regular loads). It took almost all of the 55 gallon drum of water, which is why it will be important that you recover the water when you can. The last thing I washed was the cover for the wringing bar and just hand squeezed it since it is light cotton.

I was really happy with the outcome, especially the sheets. For the sheets and the underwear I did use a third rinse that included some fabric softener, but it isn't necessary. The air alone makes things smell good. I noticed I used much less detergent and most of the water consumption was for rinsing.

The 2X4 wringer bar is attached to the back of a tree so any pulling didn't land me on my behind. It is covered with an old frayed dress shirt; an old pillowcase would work well too.

CHAPTER XII

UTILITIES

ELECTRICAL POWER - BATTERIES

Auto Battery Tester

I figure there will be additional batteries in abandoned autos if there is no gasoline. So that I do not drag home dead batteries, I found at Big Lots a "Battery Analyzer" for $2.99 that plugs into a 12 volt cigarette lighter. It will tell me if the battery is charged. (Part # 40718 - Tool and Supply of New England - 1105 Orange St., Wilmington, DE 19801). Also, if I plug the cigarette lighter into an adapter that has alligator clips, I can test my own batteries in my storage area. In addition, I have a battery charger I can run off my generator when I am using it for other purposes.

Coleman Large Tube Fluorescent 12 volt Lighting

As an alternate system for short-term emergencies, I plan to use battery powered low amperage fluorescent lights. Coleman has a large tube, fluorescent camping lantern (Model 5255) available from discount stores. It also has an option to operate only one of the two bulbs to reduce battery drain.

They are designed to run off of 8 each 1 ½ volt batteries or 2 six volt batteries. (Note: Their smaller unit is a 9 volt size using six batteries which will not work with a 12 volt auto battery.)

The great thing about the large tube model is it will also run off a 12-volt cigarette lighter adapter (Coleman Part # 5355-5201) which can be ordered from Coleman. It can be adapted with alligator clips to run off a full size auto or marine battery. (Note: For some reason, Radio Shack's 12-volt adapter will not work with this lantern).

When used with my deep charge boat battery, the two-bulb setting operated continuously for 72 hours and only reduced battery by 50 percent. If used for four hours a night on two-tube setting, it will operate for 18 days or 36 days on the one tube setting.

Other Options

In an emergency, if you cannot get florescent lights, then use marine/recreational vehicle 12 volt lights that are available from auto parts houses or most hardware stores. Many of these bulbs screw into a regular light receptacle but they use substantially more amperage.

Or you can use several battery powered auto emergency incandescent lights such as:

Magnetic Trouble Light - Manufactured by Racer's Choice - Miami, FL 33014 and available from Pep Boys (Part number 2008) for $4.99

Advanced Auto Parts has a Magnetic All Purpose Light - Manufactured by Custom Accessories - Niles, IL 60714 (Part Number 58883) for $3.84. These are 12-volt lights that plug into a cigarette lighter receptacle along with a 10-12 foot cord.

Also, at Lowes I found some neat 12 volt deck and sidewalk lighting that uses "wedge based" light bulbs (5 and 11 watts plus other wattage). They had a $5.00 plastic deck light fixture, including bulb, that would be perfect for indoor use.

Amperage Table

The following is the amperage use of each type of 12 volt lighting:

Type Bulb	Amps
Phillips 6 watt 9" fluorescent light (Coleman Lantern)	.15
Magnetic All Purpose Light (58883)	.42
Wedge based 5 watt deck lighting	.42
Wedge based 11 watt deck lighting	.92
RV 12 watt refrigerator light	1.00
Sylvania wedge base backup 18 watts light #921	1.50
Sylvania Marine/RV 50 watt #50A21/RPS	4.16

As you can see, the more watts, the faster the battery drains, so the way to go is fluorescent. Learn to manage you amperage. Now is the time to obtain your electrical fixtures and extra bulbs.

Radio

I also have an adapter from Radio Shack that I use to run my AM/FM/Short-wave and 2 meter ham radio using several methods: A 120 volt adapter, regular batteries (unlimited storage life if stored in freezer) and an auto or marine battery. Another adapter also plugs into the cigarette lighter and then adapts for direct connection to an auto battery with alligator clips.

Ham radios have neat clubs and they are all in contact with FEMA and other disaster operations. Also, per two ham operators, a marine or auto battery will be ruined when used on something with a low amperage draw like a radio. So, periodically draw down the battery some with other appliances with a larger draw, like lighting.

Try to keep batteries fully charged to maintain battery life. Marine deep cycle batteries are designed to be slowly discharged and recharged. Do not leave batteries in a discharged state and never charge inside due to gas emission.

Conclusion

I recently talked to someone who, during a tornado disaster in Raleigh, North Carolina, had all his conveniences. When all his neighbors where in the dark, he had his 12-volt deck light, a small 12-volt television, a radio and several 12-volt computer muffin fans to keep cool. (Muffin fans are cheap at Radio Shack or from flea markets and free from computer repair shops). Then when his battery became discharged, he went for a ride in his car (assuming you have gasoline) to sightsee the disaster and to charge the battery.

On the other hand, during a disaster or economic shutdown, automobiles will have no gas but may have good batteries.

TELEPHONE TIP

If electrical power is down in your area, but your phone company has alternative power or is in an area where electricity is working, your phone may still work "IF" you have a phone that doesn't require an external AC power supply.

Many cordless phones do not work if the power is out. Same for some of the feature-laden integrated phone/answering machine devices. If your phone plugs into a 110-volt electric socket in addition to the phone jack, check and see if it works when unplugged from the electrical socket. If not, go buy a cheap phone that works on just the phone jack alone, without the need of external power supply. This way you might be able to use your phone in an electrical outage.

USING KEROSENE LAMPS

The following are several email postings that explain the use of kerosene lamps. Best to use paraffin rather than kerosene to reduce odors.

Posting #1 - Kerosene Lamps

Use #2 fuel or better, water-clear kerosene; tinted/scented lamp oil gives less light, can gum up the wick or smoke up the chimney excessively. Lower grades of kerosene with higher number will work but may cause similar problems with wicks and the chimneys will be dirty sooner. Using 5 traditional lamps and a lantern 5 hours /night in the winter will use about 1 gallon/month.

Use a cheap bulb siphon and ONLY use it for kerosene. Gasoline residues in a kerosene lamp are extremely dangerous. Try not to siphon any of the sludge and throw away the last 1/2 cup in the can. Siphon outdoors to minimize problem spills. If you spill over newspaper, do not burn in wood burning stove for it may cause a chimney fire. Also, do not overfill kerosene reservoir. You need air space between the bottom of wick holder and top of the kerosene for good wicking. When installing a new wick, soak it in kerosene first. You will then burn the kerosene and not the wick. If the top of the wick is dry, only the wick will burn.

Trim the wick occasionally while using it and the first time you use it. A wick trimmed straight across will give a wide, flat-topped flame and will smoke excessively; too pointy of a wick produces a thin flame and little light. You should cut off the corners and round the top of the wick a bit. After many hours of burning, the top of the wick will get ragged and charred. The flame may even have two lobes. Trim the char off into the shape that works best for your lamp.

There are two kinds of lamp owners: those who have burned themselves and those who will. Always check before touching the chimney. You cannot see heat.

To light a kerosene lamp, remove the chimney, turn the wick up a bit, light and replace the chimney. As the wick begins to smoke, turn it down, just enough to keep from smoking. Adjust the wick for maximum light without smoking.

Extinguish a kerosene lamp by holding your hand just behind and above the chimney top. Adjust the angle of your palm to direct your breath straight down the chimney. Blow against your palm and a quick puff will blow it out.

To clean the chimney, remove soot with a facial tissue and wash in hot, soapy water. Rinse in very hot water, to which baking soda has been added to eliminate spotting and then air dry.

For wick maintenance, take stub of wick with you when buying a new one. There are circular wicks and flat wicks which come in different widths and thicknesses. One that is too thick or thin will not feed through the wick adjuster and may even damage it. It is better to use one that is too narrow than one that is the wrong thickness or width. A narrow wick will not produce as much light, obviously.

Keep spare chimneys on hand. A lamp without a chimney is worthless. Thin glass costs less but breaks easier; frosted glass diffuses the light but is less bright. Tall, thin, straight chimneys produce a thin, very bright flame, while bulbous chimneys produce a wider flame and maybe more total light. Different chimney styles means adjusting to trimming the wick differently.

You may eventually have to put on a new wick adjuster through normal usage or by damage by improper wick. You will have to replace the whole burner. Keep an extra one or two on hand. The best lamp has a heavy glass base that allows you to see how much kerosene is left. The weight of the base gives stability.

Aladdin lamps are much more expensive than traditional lamps. They use pressure to volatilize the kerosene and a mantle to distribute and intensify the flame. They put out twice the light but also use twice as much kerosene as a traditional lamp and the mantles have to be replaced frequently. The parts of one model of Aladdin lamp may not be interchangeable with one another.

PROPANE LIGHTS AND APPLIANCES

If you have a large home bulk propane tank, I am told propane gas grills will not operate properly from them because of two regulators in series. There is a main home tank regulator and the regulator on your BBQ grill. So you need a special low pressure stove burner, such as the "Cajun Cooker". I find that N.H. Northern - 800-222-5381 has an economical propane burner unit that operates from the 20 pound/5 gallon tank or your home bulk tank.

As a back up, I also made a tee off my primary 250-gallon propane tank (after the regulator) so I can feed my generator and portable propane surface burner. I have recently added an additional 250 gallon tank next to my other tank with a separate cut off so it will only be used in an emergency.

From a recreation vehicle dealer I acquired a wall mounted propane light ($50.00) to provide extra lighting if needed.

To operate my propane Coleman camping cook stove and lanterns, I bought the Coleman distribution tree from a discount store that allows the 20 pound/5-gallon propane tank to be my fuel source rather than the expensive smaller camping cylinders. I also have the 8-foot hose, made by Coleman, that allows more flexibility.

Many building supply companies offer natural gas and propane ventless space heaters. I run a separate propane line from my 250-gallon tank to the space heater with a cut off with a cap. A flexible propane rated line (available from from most propane dealers for around a $1.25 a foot) could be run to operate off an exterior 20-pound/5-gallon tank if your home is not on propane. Be sure to obtain all the flared brass connections you need and assemble and test it now.

To insure my safety when using CO emitting appliances, I own a battery powered CO detector that detects both low and high levels of CO.

I have a brass coupler that lets you fill Coleman camping sized cylinders using 20-pound/5-gallon propane tanks. What a barter item one would have exchanging full cylinders for empty ones. Available N.H. Northern (800-222-5381) - Item # 17264-C131 $15.99 plus shipping.

How to Purchase New 20-Pound/5-Gallon Propane Tanks for $3.00

In every major disaster when the power goes out, everyone uses his or her patio gas grill to cook, boil water, etc. Suddenly there is a shortage of propane. So I believe everyone needs enough extra tanks for their use, to help family and close friends. In addition, a full propane tank would make a prized bartering tool. As you have learned, these tanks can be adapted for providing heat, light and connected to a separate stove burner unit.

If you have not purchased a new patio grill lately, they now have stove top burner option on one side separate from the grill area. Now you can grill or cook using a normal gas burner. Unfortunately, the new grills have an ACME/OPD valve connector that will not work on your old style tank. As you will see, this is good for you.

New empty propane tanks can be purchased for $25.00 or more, but I obtained mine for $3.00 each. Here is how I did it: In my area it costs $9.95 to refill a propane tank or, at Home Depot, it costs $12.95 with an exchange of your old tank. I found that the stores that refill tanks sometimes have an accumulation of the "old style" tanks that people have decided not to upgrade to an ACME/OPD valve, the tanks are defective or have passed their expiration dates.

So, after visiting four locations, I recovered a dozen used old-style tanks for free. Then I found out that Home Depot has no restrictions on what kind of tank you could exchange for the new ACME/OPD tanks and at no extra cost.

After the exchange, I have all new-style filled tanks that I exchanged for $12.95 each that only cost me $3.00 for each empty tank ($12.95-$9.95).

Be aware that the old style tanks will not work on a new style grill but an old style grill will work with a new style tank.

CHAPTER XIII

FUEL STORAGE

GASOLINE STORAGE

My research and development corporate fuels source told me that gasoline, even with stabilizers, will last only one year or so.

The key is to keep the fuel cool per Georgia USDA Fuels and Measures. They regularly have problems with new combines being shipped with just enough gas to load and unload them and the heat ruins the gasoline. The message is that a small volume of gasoline has a larger temperature variance than a large one and will go bad by reaching high temperatures.

The EPA regulates stored gas in an underground tank which can leak. There are substantial fines if a leak is found. EPA states that there are no burying of tank restrictions for agricultural use.

My R&D source said to only store gasoline in metal containers. He states that if a 55-gallon drum is used (which he recommended against), be sure to keep it sheltered, sealed tight and allow a 10 percent head space for expansion.

A local distributor says gasoline expands more than diesel. He also said to be sure to keep the drum covered so rain cannot enter gas by collecting on top and be sure to use a stabilizer. Stabilizers reduce oxidation and contain a biocide and should be added immediately when fuel is purchased.

I was told one can smell when gas has been affected by oxygen and goes bad. It was only described as unusual non-gasoline smell. Others have said it smells like varnish. The USDA states that the bad gas can have a sulfur-like smell and looks dull. Good gas has a sparkle and looks fluorescent. Older gas also gets darker.

Winter gas is different than summer gasoline. The wrong gas used at the wrong time could cause stalls and vapor locks.

I also talked to someone who had a parent who was a missionary and that they stored gasoline for up to a year due to irregularity of delivery. It was stored in a plastic tank. Each time gas was pumped, the first gallon was put in a clear container to check for water. If found, the gasoline was poured off and the water dumped. After talking to someone else, I found that the gasoline in other countries does not have the oxidizers we use for cleaner burning and to meet pollution laws and, therefore, third world countries can store gasoline much, much longer and with less restrictions. Our gasoline begins to deteriorate after only several months.

If gasoline is transported, the container needs to be grounded because a static spark from the tank to the ground could be the end of your storage career. This is especially true with trucks with plastic beds. I was told to ground the tank on the ground with a metal rod.

I also read the following email about Sta-bil. "I experimented with stored gas last winter. I know I did it right. I put Sta-bil in to their directions and stored for nine months. I had to re-build every carburetor I had. Gummed everything up hopelessly."

So this is where I am on the issue. I need gasoline for my automobile and my tiller, so I am planning on using a 55-

gallon metal drum filled with gas and a PRI (stabilizer). I will keep it in barn with my other fuels. I am also buying a dozen 5 gallon gas cans, made by Rubbermaid and available from Home Depot for a little over $6.00 each. They will be very portable and I will store them in my smaller shaded storage building, add a PRI stabilizer and I will then rotate them on a regular basis.

In every disaster where I have been, gasoline becomes the most desired item after water. When there's no power, no gas is pumped.

Finally, I found an excellent article about fuel storage by Ralph E. Lewis and a product produced by Power Research Inc. (PRI)

FUEL DEGRADATION STORAGE - ARE YOU PREPARED?

We've seen gasoline have shelf life as little as a month - particularly if it is subjected to heat and moisture. Diesel fuels fare a little better, but not much. Most all diesel fuel, including the EPA's mandated low sulfur version, has a shelf life of from 3-to-6 months. Again, this varies widely. Recently we tracked a diesel fuel produced at a refinery in Texas to its final destination in Florida. When tested at the refinery the same day it was produced, the fuel barely met the specification for stability. After being stored, pumped into a coastal tanker, offloaded at Port Everglades, stored again, delivered to the fuel jobber, and finally to the customer, 23 days had passed. Again the fuel was tested. This "fresh" fuel now tested out of "spec". To make matters worse, one oil company survey indicates that at least 50 percent of the gasoline sold today is substandard.

On a small scale, there are always 5-gallon military surplus "Jerry-cans". They are inexpensive and durable. But you'll need a lot of them if your fuel supply needs are great. Next option is auxiliary tanks for vehicles and pickups. Many truck supply companies manufacture tanks that fit in pickup beds. Consider 55-gallon steel drums. These must be stored in a well-ventilated area away from heat.

"Poly" drums - the type sold for water storage - are made of high-density plastic and should not be used to store fuel. Over time, the fuel will react with the plastic (a hydrocarbon) and gradually deteriorate the drum interior.

Large surface storage tanks with capacities of 250 gallons plus are the best alternative. Many commercial fuel suppliers or "jobbers" that dispense gas, diesel and home heating oil lease or sell these tanks, or can direct you to a good source.

If you live in an urban area, small 5-gallon nylon or metal storage cans will have to do. If you have access to, or own, rural property, then above-ground tankage is the answer. Place your tank in a cool, shaded area if outdoors. Best yet, put your tank in an indoor, covered location. Remember that heat from sunlight will speed the oxidative process in stored fuel and temperature swings will cause condensation to build, resulting in water accumulation in tank bottoms. Whatever tank you use, make sure it is equipped with a valve on the tank bottom so that you can periodically drain any water accumulation.

Keep your tank topped off - leaving about 5 -10 percent of capacity free for headspace. The same holds true for steel drums. This minimizes condensation, yet gives room for fuel to expand and contract with temperature variances.

Invest in a good quality spin-on fuel filter that separates water. Put this on the output line from the tank - whether you are using gasoline or diesel fuel. They make small ones for small tanks, and they are commonly available at marine supply stores. Keep a good supply of spare filter cartridges on hand.

Additionally, avoid the use of copper or any copper brazing on your tank. Minute particles of copper can contaminate the fuel - and these few particles can actually accelerate fuel deterioration.

How long can PRI keep fuel fresh? This depends on the original condition of the fuel. While tests indicate that PRI can keep fuels fresh, in many instances, for 10 years and more, fuel should be dosed with PRI every 6-12 months for maximum benefit. If your fuel is already in poor condition, do not worry. PRI-D for diesel, and PRI-G for gasoline have also demonstrated an uncanny capability to restore very old, stale fuels to refinery fresh conditions.

In one extreme case, a doubting client took a 15-year old sample of some very gummy and malodorous gasoline from a junkyard car in New Hampshire. He sent the sample to Saybolt Laboratories in Boston for analysis. Predictably, the fuel was completely unusable when tested for oxidation stability. When treated with PRI-G and re-tested , this bad fuel was completely restored to refinery freshness.

The key to PRI chemistry is our proprietary enhanced thermal stability chemistry. This unique chemistry is not available in the "consumer" additives at auto parts stores and marine and RV supply outfits. We've had many of these products independently tested and, not surprisingly, the majority of these "stabilizers" do little or nothing to preserve fuels. Some even make the fuel worse. The fact that some manufacturers heavily dilute these formulas with common solvent carriers - reducing their strength - is evidenced by the poor treatment rates of these products. This also makes them very expensive on a per treated gallon basis.

Many people are unaware that about 85 percent of our business is treating the heavy "bunker" fuel oil consumed by the world's great merchant and cruise shipping companies. This fuel is of a far worse quality than diesel and gasoline, yet PRI's thermal stability chemistry prevents hard carbon deposits from forming on critical engine components, saving these companies hundreds of thousands of dollars annually by dramatically reducing engine wear rates and improving fuel economy.

Also, when I asked PRI's marketing director about how long PRI would preserve freshness of fuels, his reply was, "PRI will take fuel to 5-10 years of freshness. You can retreat after that time as well and keep it going for another couple of years or more. PRI itself is good indefinitely when stored in a stoppered container. It will turn darker over time, but will remain just as effective as when new. I'm actually still using product that is five years old, in bottles with a design we phased out in 1994. Works great!"

Power Research Inc. has made arrangements with Camper's World centers to make PRI available to the public. Contact Camper's World: 800-993-2212. 16 fluid ounces treats 250 gallons. PRI-G Gasoline Treatment - Catalog #16028 - $12.99 plus shipping. PRI-D Diesel Treatment - Catalog #16027 - $12.99 plus shipping.

CHAPTER XIV

THE NARROW HOLE LATRINE

The narrow hole latrine is the most innovative method I have seen. Its source is from the "Dwelling Portably Newsletter."

When only a few people are camping and spending just a few days in one spot, "cat holes" are sufficient. Dig a hole a few inches deep in the soil with a stick, rock or empty can. After use, fill in the hole. Dig a new hole each time. But, at a long occupied home camp, cat holes will soon use up all of the adjacent easily-dug ground.

The traditional disposal method at group camps is the wide-hole latrine. One large hole is dug and covered with a sheet of plywood with a hole in. Unfortunately, it doesn't offer sanitary disposal. The wide-hole fails, first, because most feces are stickier than most dirt (or ashes). Also, most of the feces pile up under the hole whereas most of the dirt that is sprinkled on the pile slides down the sides of the pile. Consequently some feces remains exposed and there are always odors and flies.

A solution we have discovered is the narrow-hole latrine. Dig a hole about eight inches in diameter and a couple of feet deep. The ideal tool might be a post hole digger. If the ground is soft, a narrow bladed shovel works fairly well, one without much angle between blade and handle is best.

After each use, the feces are covered with dirt. This is easy in a narrow-holer, because there is nowhere for the dirt to slide. With complete coverage there's no odor and no flies, which encourages the next user to also cover completely. Stop using the hole while a few inches of space remain and fill this with dirt. Tamp down firmly, pile more dirt on top and stamp that down. This discourages animals from digging it up.

Finally sprinkle on some dead leaves to absorb the impact of raindrops and prevent erosion. At home camp, we space the holes a foot or two apart and take dirt from a new hole for covering the hole in use. So, by the time one hole is full, a new hole is ready.

CHAPTER XV

LOOTING - NEIGHBORS CRUISING FOR YOUR GOODS

Each year disasters shred thousands of homes and mingle the tatters of lumber, drywall, shingles and roof tiles into one sickening blanket of scrap building materials. As if dealing with a major disaster was not enough, I have found looting to be on the increase. It is interesting to note now, and it was appalling to observe then, that the majority of the victims were demanding that the "government--or someone--do something." The prevailing rationale was that the victims were not responsible for their own safety and welfare. Unfortunately, the magnitude of this disaster shut down an already cumbersome governmental support system upon which they were depending.

It was during Hurricane Hugo in the Carolinas that I first observed the extent of looting during a disaster. Of the hundreds of victims that I have dealt with, most had lost something to looters. Pillage even occurred in the rural areas. Then came Hurricane Andrew in south Florida. There the storm related damage estimates reached 20 billion dollars in property damage, 250,000 people homeless, 35,000 in shelters and 1.3 million lacking power--one of the costliest disasters ever in the United States. Here, looting took on a life of its own. Many times whole families, including children, could be seen pushing shopping carts full of merchandise they had stolen.

Unfortunately, thieves and looters seek out those who have cash or goods. Most victims are too intent on making a purchase or solving their immediate crisis to be aware that others are watching them. They falsely assume no one could be so cruel as to take from those who had already lost most, or all, of their possessions.

In large disasters, the National Guard will furnish some security, but the extensive debris blocking the roads will delay it. The extent of a large damage area makes the efforts even less effective. Also, the expedient focusing of National Guard activity mainly on town centers leaves rural residents unserved, disgruntled and very vulnerable to attack. During Hurricane Andrew, the Assistant City Manager of Homestead, Florida reported that he had a hundred National Guard next to the city hall. Every time he tried to direct them to a problem area, he was told they needed approval from higher up which took hours and sometimes days. Unfortunately, there was a severe shortage of on-site leadership.

Before the National Guard's presence is known, looting is always widespread. In many cases, "neighbors" do the plundering from the next block. In one complex, during Hurricane Hugo, three scavengers gained entry into a number of the evacuated apartments. But when they began to pry one door open, one remaining occupant threatened to shoot. The looters then kicked in the door of the next apartment and ransacked it rather than face someone who was armed.

During one disaster, with no streetlights, pitch-blackness prevailed at night. It was frightening to see many people milling around after dark as both a result of and cause for anxiety. In one suburban area, the National Guard was unable to enforce an imposed curfew as people experienced the boredom and anxiety that rapidly sets in when normal patterns are disrupted. In some low-income areas, the bars were in full swing by noon, and by dusk, bands of drunken men were moving out into urban areas looking for something to do.

I recall a fright I experienced one evening when returning late to my motel during Hurricane Hugo's recovery operations. I made a wrong turn and found myself lost in the inner city after curfew. When I paused at the first intersection, several people brushed my car checking for an unlocked door.

I was fortunate, for they might have broken out a window and crawled in. Needless to say, I did not slow down at other intersections. During Hurricane Andrew, looting was common place and accepted as a way of life. One victim from an upper class neighborhood told me, "I was shunned by my neighbors because I rejected an offer to cruise for goods."

As Fred Taylor, Metro-Dade police director said, "The looting has occurred in areas made vulnerable in the storm. That's mostly homes on main roads, convenience stores and strip shopping malls. The takers included young people, old people and people with little kids. Some had guns."

In another situation, a looter was questioned about his looting as he carried out a television. He said, "I'm not looting - I need this television."

It was clear the looters knew the inability of law enforcement to handle masses of looters. "The police know we are here," said one female in her late teens, who declined to identify herself. She was pushing a shopping cart overflowing with clothes through the shattered plate glass window of a flooded T.J. Max store.

Police confessed they had more important worries. "Frankly, the priority is not property," one said. "We're only handling life-threatening situations." What he said is probably true, for the victims I worked with who lost most of their personal goods or business inventory due to looting saw very few arrests. Drug stores and veterinary clinics were especially vulnerable for drug theft.

But justice prevailed in one interesting instance. As the crowd cheered, a woman was handcuffed and led away from the Royal Palm Ice Company. Her crime: Trying to cut in the line, nearly a quarter-mile long and 5,000 strong, waiting to buy bags of ice from the back of several trailer trucks. A dozen Miami police had been on duty at the icehouse since 7 a.m. The wait was at least four hours; the cost for a 4-pound bag was $5. "They are fighting in ice lines all over town," one policeman said.

One thing I have learned is that your protection will be your prior planning. During the LA riots, a major portion of those injured were going to get food or water. If they had been prepared to be self-supporting for two weeks, the danger would have passed. In addition, I have yet to see a loss due to looting occur to anyone who was prepared to defend his or her property.

During Hurricane Andrew, peaceful citizens packed guns to protect their flattened homes, as looters pushed shopping carts through downtown Homestead, Florida. I talked with a lawyer who was a victim and who had been away in another city during the actual storm. His neighbors had called him and told him to buy shotgun ammunition. Being somewhat passive and not knowledgeable about guns, he went to a gun store and asked for ammunition. The storeowner asked him what "load" he wanted. Then, noting the unsureness, added, "Is it to be used for rabbits?" The victim replied, "Well not actually--Larger." "For deer?" the owner asked. The victim stammered that he was from Homestead where they had looters. The storeowner responded: "Well, why didn't you say so in the first place? Here is the load you need for looters." The homeowner told me that he now cherishes his right to protect himself.

During Hurricane Hugo, prepared neighborhoods barricaded their block. Home watch guards worked in shifts during the day and night. This system was very effective. Active involvement with neighbors now will aid in future group preparedness actions.

One storeowner I met was the only retailer in his shopping center that was not looted. His solution was a generator for light, a cooler for food and drink, a comfortable chair located in his doorway while on guard and a shotgun. He never had to even point it, for all looters gave him full berth while seeking easier spoils.

The larger disasters experienced in this decade continue to breed looting. Unfortunately, because of the magnitude of many disasters, the support agencies were unable to adequately handle the effects. There was confusion and false starts on the part of federal and local agencies. Many victims had cause to feel helpless and become angry toward the powers in control.

CONCLUSION

Yes, food storage is truly a wise investment. I once saw an Associated Press release where a scientist stated that starvation would be the number one killer in the next world war.

Then, a few years ago the Social Security Administration predicted that within the next 60 years, a $70.00 grocery bill (which only fifteen years ago was $25.00) will run over $1,500.00. By storing foods now, you hedge against inflation and shortages and those savings are tax free. So, invest in your future and not just in the bank.

This book will get you started. For many, the planning time is over and you must begin with step one. Storing food for emergencies can become a rewarding enterprise, even if disasters never demand using it. Remember that even if you never need your reserves, they are an insurance policy and an investment.

Food value goes up 5-10 percent a year and the gain is tax-free. If you don't use your reserves after a period of time, then donate to a local shelter and take the appreciated tax write-off. It is a win-win situation, but you must begin now!

In any survival situation, knowledge and advance preparation are crucial, although loss cannot be completely prevented nor predicted. Yet, understanding the tendencies of a natural disaster can enable one to become prepared physically and emotionally. Surely the mistakes made and the lessons learned from past disasters will not soon be forgotten--or will disasters continue to put unprepared people into desperate straits?

APPENDIX A

A PERSONAL NOTE FROM KEN

Many people increase their faith in God during difficult times. Those of us who have been in war refer to it as "foxhole religion" or "There are no atheists in foxholes."

It was in Viet Nam that my testing began. The duty days were fourteen hours long, seven days a week. There was just enough time to finish guard mount, eat, wash if there was water, and go to sleep. It seemed that before I was even settled in bed, it was morning and I awoke while laying in a puddle of sweat from the hot, humid night before. Many nights I would be awakened by several rapid firings of a 40 millimeter cannon next to my position, usually a firefight caused by something tripping a warning flare or a claymore mine.

And so it went, day in and day out causing the stress to build. Some cannot deal with the separation from loved ones and the constant fear for their lives. Early in my tour, our "point man" armed with a twelve gauge shotgun "cracked" and proceeded to shoot up the compound. Later we had a Captain who, after six months in country, went on R&R (Rest & Recuperation) to meet his wife in Hawaii. When he got off the plane, she handed him divorce papers. The night he returned to his unit he was found with a 45 caliber pistol stuffed in his belt and a knife in his hand trying to attack his bunkmate.

In my case, I had an emotional release outlet. About once a week, as I looked down the valley we were protecting, I would hear the ever present gunfire. It was usually punctuated with mortar or tracked anti-aircraft guns we used on enemy ground forces. As I surveyed my fear, frustration, and hopelessness, I would become overwhelmed and sob for what seemed like forever. Then composure would surface and I would be OK for several days.

If only I could survive this tour and return to the states! With the survival skills and independence I had so intensely acquired, I could deal with anything. Fortunately, my life was spared and I returned home.

Working as a District Marketing Manager with Ford Motor Company, covering Maryland, Delaware and Washington, DC., I was on the "fast track" leading to the "Crystal Palace" in Detroit. I had a nice home, an executive position, and numerous material possessions, but I was dissatisfied with my work, other people, and life in general. So I tried climbing one step higher on the corporate ladder and accepted a position with FMC as a Regional Manager over 13 states. This meant a marketing staff, a larger title, more money, increased travel, and deeper frustration.

My disillusion bottomed-out one day while I was on an automobile trip from Baltimore to Pittsburgh. I felt compelled to review my life since college. With a degree in Industrial Design and an MBA from Auburn University, I had been a design engineer with Lock-heed; a business consultant; a marketing manager with Ford Motor Company; and now I was a regional manager with FMC, a large Fortune 100 company. I was supposed to be thankful for my professional growth and lifestyle, but, instead, I felt empty.

Tracing my path, regardless of the increased income and assets I acquired, I sensed there was still something I needed to feel successful and satisfied. I had finally talked my way into a job in which I knew I was not meeting the performance criteria, and there were problems in my marriage. The reality of losing control over my life became more depressing. I knew no real happiness and could not achieve any sense of peace in my life.

My former assumption that happiness is related to success had been quickly altered one day on a plane flight as I sat beside the captain of a pleasure-boat belonging to a very wealthy businessman—so successful that his pleasure boat was 150 feet long and had a full time crew of three. Such a craft symbolized everything I had been striving for in my life. I was talking to someone who was next to that wealth and success, who could tell me first hand about what it was really like at the top. After we talked for a while, I asked him: "Your employer is very successful; what is it like at the top?"

The man was thoughtful for a minute before he said: "Let me answer it this way. Do you know what my employer does on Friday night? He comes down to the boat, and we sit around and get drunk together." There was a profound silence while my dreams crumbled—it was unnerving to realize that success did not guarantee happiness.

Later on that day as I was driving toward Pittsburgh, my considerations were halted by a roadblock on the turnpike; a blizzard had shut off all access to the Pittsburgh area. As I started back to Baltimore, hopelessness overwhelmed me. I concluded that life was not worth the effort, and I needed to "punch out." It seemed that my only solution was to commit suicide. Exploring ways to do it, I decided to hit one of the bridge supports. Then I thought of the direct possibility, with the way my luck was going, that I could not do it right and I would only be crippled.

I had gone to church all my life and was basically a good person, but here I was, brooding in deepest despair. Suddenly the voice of a radio preacher broke through my desolation, and I heard him say, "If you have reached the top and find there is nothing there; if you do not have peace in your life, try God." It seemed he was speaking directly to me! The preacher said: "Put Jesus to the test and see if he can straighten out your life."

I knew I didn't have anything left to lose so I pulled off the turnpike and gave myself up to following the man's clear instructions. I remembered John 3:16. Then I prayed: "Jesus, if you can straighten me out, then I need you in my life. I believe you died for my sins, and you can give me everlasting life. I accept you as my personal savior." Then it happened! My letting go of my life in a simple act of faith caused a peace to flow over me that I can't explain. I felt as if a two-hundred pound backpack was lifted off my shoulders.

Since that day, my life has had its difficulties as well as good times, but through them, God has provided me a "peace that passes all understanding." I have no more fears nor worries because I know that no matter what happens, now I have a special Presence supporting and guiding me. Not only did I receive inner healing and eternal salvation; my relationship with my family also began to be wonderful.

That small town radio preacher in Pennsylvania will never know the impact his simple message had on my life, my family, and my two children! Now I want my simple message to help others. My goal is to know the God of the Bible intimately, to read and study His blueprint for living (the Bible) daily, to talk with Him in prayer, and to find his direction for my life.

As we see the present foundations of our world crumbling, we can find peace and strength. Remember Philippines 4:6, 7 says: "Do not be anxious about anything, but in everything through prayer and petition, with thanksgiving, make your requests to God. And the peace of God, which transcends all understanding, will guard your hearts and minds in Christ Jesus". Someone who has promised never to leave or forsake us–Rest in peace; God is awake.

Ken Larson

Bible Verses That Explain God's Plan For Life and Eternity: God's love (John 3:16). We have all sinned against God (Romans 3:23). The penalty for our sin is death–physical and spiritual (Romans 6:23). Christ died in our place and rose from the dead (Romans 5:8). Finally, all you need to do is ask Christ alone for forgiveness and eternal life and a peace that passes all understanding will flood your life.

APPENDIX B

WELDED WIRE FISH TRAP CONSTRUCTION PLANS

Trap constructed from one inch welder wire

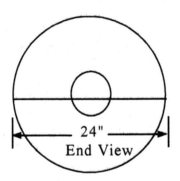

24"
End View

Hinged
Catch Removal Door

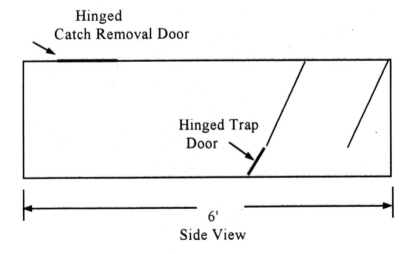

Hinged Trap
Door

6'
Side View

CLOVER-LEAF PANFISH TRAP

Made from 1/2" hardware cloth. Purchase a 3'X5' piece
to make whole trap.

SLAT FISH TRAP CONSTRUCTION PLANS

Basic dimensions are 12" X 12" X 4'. Wood frame ends surrounded by thin, lateral wood slats. Use 1/4" spacing between slats. A wood throat is nailed to the ends with a plastic throat in the center. The plastic throats are available from the suppliers listed in the fish trap chapter.

Slat Fish Trap with side (fish removal) panel removed

APPENDIX C

Drying of Vegetables and Fruit

Vegetable	Preparation	Treatment Before Drying (choose one)	Time (min)	Average drying time Oven (hrs)	Dehydrator (hrs)	Test for dryness (Cool before testing)
Artichokes, globe	Cut hearts into 1/8 inch strips.	Heat in boiling solution of ¾ cups water and 1 tablespoon lemon juice.	6-8	4-7	2-3	Brittle
Asparagus	Wash thoroughly, cut large tips in half.	steam— / water—	4-5 / 3½-4½	3-4	1-2 / ¾-4½	Leathery to brittle
Beans, snap	Wash thoroughly. Cut lengthwise or into 1 inch pieces.	steam—	3½-4	3-6	3-4	Brittle dark green to brownish color
Beets	Cook as for serving. Peel. Cut into shoestring strips 1/8 inch thick.	Already cooked, No further blanching required.		3-5	2-3	Brittle dark red to black color
Broccoli	Trim cut as for serving. Wash thoroughly. Quarter stalks lengthwise.	steam— / water—	4-5 / 3-4	3-4	3-4	Brittle
Brussels sprouts	Cut in half lengthwise through stem.	steam— / water—	6-7 / 4½-5½	4-5	2-3	Brittle
Cabbage	Remove outer leaves, quarter and core. Cut into strips 1/8 inch thick.	steam— / water—	2½-3 / 1½-2	1-3	1-2	Brittle
Carrots	Use only crisp, tender carrots. Wash thoroughly. Trim and peel. Cut in slices or strips 1/8 inch thick.	steam— / water—	6-7 / 4-6	4-5	3-4	Tough leathery
Cauliflower	Prepare as for serving.	steam— / water—	4-5 / 3-4	4-6	2-3	Tough to brittle
Celery (both stalks and leaves may be dried)	Wash stalks and leaves thoroughly. Slice stalks lengthwise.	steam— / water—	3-4 / 2-3	3-4	2-3	Brittle
Corn	Select tender, mature sweet corn. Husk and trim. Cut from cob after blanching.	steam— / water—	5-6 / 4-5	2-3	1-2	Dry, brittle

Vegetable	Preparation	Method				Test
Eggplant	Wash thoroughly. Peel and cut into ¼ inch slices or cubes.	steam— water—	4 3	3-5	2-3	Brittle
Greens (chard, kale, turnip, spinach)	Use only young tender leaves. Wash and trim very thoroughly.	steam— water—	3-5 2-3	2½-3½	2-3½	Brittle
Mushrooms (Use only young, medium sized, freshly picked "Gills" that are pink colored and free of insects and black discoloration.)	Scrub thoroughly. Dry small mushrooms whole or sliced. Peel and slice large mushrooms.	No blanching needed.		4-5	3-4	Tough to brittle
Okra	Wash, trim, and slice crosswise into ¼ inch disks.	steam— water—	4-5 3-4	3-4	2-3	Tough to brittle
Onions	Wash and remove outer paper shells. Trim and slice ¼ inch thick.	No blanching needed.		3-5	1-3	Brittle
Peas, green	Use young, tender peas of a sweet variety. Shell.	steam— water—	3 2	3-4	2-3	Hard, wrinkled
Peppers and Pimientos	Wash, stem, and core. Cut into strips or rings 3/8 inch thick.	No blanching needed.		3-5	3½-4	Brittle
Potatoes, white	Wash, peel and cut into shoestring stiprs ¼ inch thick or slices 1¼ inch thick	steam— water—	6-8 5-6	4-6	2-4	Brittle
Pumpkin and Hubbard Squash	Quarter, remove seeds and pit, cut into 1 inch strips, and peel. Slice strips crosswise ¼ inch thick.	steam— water—	8-10 —	4-5	3-4	Flesh pliable, slightly sticky but not wet
Squash, summer	Wash, trim, and cut into ¼ inch slices.	steam— water—	4 3	4-6	3-3½	Brittle
Tomatoes	Wash, peel, and cut into sections or slices ¼ inch thick.	steam— water—	2-3	6-8	4-6	Slightly leathery

Fruit	Preparation	Treatment			Test for Dryness
Apples	Peel, trim, core and cut into slices or rings ¼ inch thick. Treat with ascorbic acid solution to prevent browning.	—Sulfur 30-60 minutes, depending on size of pieces —Dip in sulfur solution —Steam blanch 10 minutes	3-4	6-12	Soft, pliable, no moist area in center when cut
Apricots	Wash, do not peel. Cut in half and remove pit. Treat with ascorbic acid solution to prevent browning.	—Sulfur 1-2 hours, depending on size of pieces with pit cavity up. —Dip in sulfur solution —Steam blanch 5-10 minutes —Blanch in hot syrup (equal parts of corn syrup, sugar, and water).	2-3	18-24	Same as apples
Berries	Wash, sort and leave whole except halve or slice strawberries.	—No treatment —Steam blanch ½-1 minute —Crack skins by dipping 15-30 seconds in boiling water then in cold water.	1-2	24	Hard rattle when shaken on tray, no moisture when crushed.
Cherries	Wash, sort, leave whole or stem and remove pit.	—No treatment*—Crack skins by dipping 15-20 seconds in boiling water then in cold water —Blanch in hot syrup.	2-3	6-8	Leathery but slightly sticky
Figs	Select fully ripe fruit. Immature fruit may sour before drying. Wash or clean whole fruit with damp cloth. Leave small fruit, whole, otherwise cut in half.	—Crack skin on whole fruit by dipping 30-45 seconds in boiling water then in cold water. —Sulfur light colored varieties. —Steam blanch cut fruit 20 minutes. —Blanch in hot syrup.	3-5	6-12	Flesh pliable, slightly sticky, but not wet.
Grapes	Wash, sort and stem seedless varieties. Cut other varieties in half and remove seeds.	—No treatment. —Dip in boiling water 15-30 seconds then in cold water to crack skins.	2-4	8-12	Raisin-like texture but not wet in center.
Nectarines and Peaches	Peel if desired. Cut in half and remove pit. Leave in halves or cut into quarters or slices. Treat with ascorbic acid solution to prevent browning.	—Sulfur halves and quarters 2 hours, slices 1 hour —Steam blanch halves and quarters 15-20 minutes, slices 5 minutes. —If blanched sulfur 90 and 30 minutes respectively.	3-5	15-20	Soft pliable, no moisture when cut or squeezed.

	Preparation			Test for doneness
Pears	Peel, cut in half and remove core. Leave in halves or cut into quarters or slices. Treat with ascorbic acid solution to prevent browning.	–Sulfur as for peaches. –Steam blanch 5-20 minutes depending upon size of pieces. –Blanch in hot syrup.	3-5	15-20	Soft, pliable, no moisture when cut or squeezed.
Persimmons	Use firm fruit of long, soft varieties and fully ripe fruit of round drier varieties. Peel and quarter on slice using stainless steel knife.	–Do not sulfur. –No treatment. –Steam blanch in hot syrup.	3-5	12-15	Light to medium brown color, flesh pliable but not sticky.
Plums	Wash, sort, and dry whole if small, otherwise, into halves or slices.	–Dip whole fruit in boiling water 30-45 seconds then in cold water to crack skins. –Steam blanch halves 15 minutes, slices 5 minutes –Sulfur whole fruit 2 hours, slices 1 hour.	3-4	6-8	Soft, pliable, no moisture when cut or squeezed.

Note: Set temperatures at 140 degrees for oven and dehydrator drying. Sun drying requires temperatures of 85-100 degrees, therefore sun drying of vegetables not recommended.

INDEX

Animal grains	163
Barter items	58
Canned foods	35
Cattail	134
Commodities	48
Dehydrator drying	59
Diatomaceous earth	182
Dried foods nutritive value	84
Dried foods storing	80
Drying food methods	63
Drying food equipment	62
Drying foods	59
Edible insects	149
Eggs	184
Evacuation provisions	44
Feed grade grains	161
Fish traps	117
Food drying	58
Food inventory extension	37
Food inventory list	39, 42
Food, low moisture	47
Food self life	41, 54
Food shortages	30, 185
Food spoilage	61
Food storage	29, 34
Foraging	133
Fuel storage	203
Gardening	54
Gasoline storage	203
Grapes	140
Greenbrier	143
Insects as food	147

Kerocene   197
Latrine   209
Laundry   188
Looting   212
Personal note   217
Pigeon breeds   110
Pigeon cleanliness   109
Pigeon facilities   104
Pigeon feeds   114·
Pigeon lofts   106
Pigeon nest boxes   113
Pigeons   101
Propane   199
Rabbits   85
Recipes   165
Self-sufficiency   159
Seven major mistakes   176
Three grain storage system   161
Trappers grub stake   180
Two pantry inventory system   37
Utilities   194
Water conservation   25
Waterproofing   150
Water purification   20
Water saving ideas   187
Water sources   18
Water storage   11
Water storage containers   13
Water storage precautions   17
Water storage tips   17
Wild foods   133

GOD'S FREE HARVEST
Successful Harvesting of Nature's Free Foods

This amazing guide is for anyone who enjoys nature. You will learn how to reduce trips to the corner grocery store, garden with wild foods, learn to pick trailside snacks and just have fun while camping using wild foods for dinner. Wild foods are free, nutritious, natural, organic and they grow unattended outside your backdoor. Includes many detailed illustrations and 41 full page photos. 240 pages. $12.95

NUCLEAR EMERGENCY
How to Protect Your Family from Radiation

Your unique guide to disaster preparedness. Understanding the effects of nuclear plant meltdowns, nuclear terrorism and nuclear weapons is critical to your family's safety! Now you can learn what could happen, how to respond, radiation shielding and shelter construction. Cancer is a serious risk–Are You Ready? 144 pages. 52 photos and illustrations. $10.95

NATURE'S FREE PHARMACY
Home Remedies Using Nature's Healing Herbs

We can all benefit from a knowledge of herbal medicine for healing minor medical problems. Discover yourself the health benefits of free, natural wild herbs without the side effects of costly drugs. Modern medicine is discovering that herbal remedies really work. Now you can learn how natural healing herbs can help you. 160 pages. 40 illustrations. $10.95

Postage & Handling: First book $2.00. Additional books $1.00 each.

Rhema Publishing, Inc.
P.O. Box 789
Suwanee, GA 30024
770-932-6991